Technology Law

What Every Business (And Business-Minded Person) Needs to Know

Mark Grossman

The Scarecrow Press, Inc.
Lanham, Maryland, and Oxford
2004

SCARECROW PRESS, INC.

Published in the United States of America
by Scarecrow Press, Inc.
A wholly owned subsidiary of
The Rowman & Littlefield Publishing Group, Inc.
4501 Forbes Boulevard, Suite 200, Lanham, Maryland 20706
www.scarecrowpress.com

PO Box 317
Oxford
OX2 9RU, UK

British Library Cataloguing in Publication Information Available

Library of Congress Cataloging-in-Publication Data

Grossman, Mark, 1957–
    Technology law : what every business (and business-minded person)
needs to know / Mark Grossman.
        p.   cm.
    Includes index.
    ISBN 0-8108-4738-8 (pbk. : alk. paper)
    1. Computers—Law and legislation—United States.   2. Internet—Law
and legislation—United States.   3. Electronic commerce—Law and
legislation—United States.   4. Technology and law—United States.   I.
Title.
    KF390.5.C6 G76   2004
    343.7309'944—dc22   2003017047

Contents

Preface

Technology has always fascinated me. Gemini, Apollo, and Star Trek all captivated me as a kid. I managed to marry both law and technology by becoming a tech lawyer.

I had always wanted to write. I started in 1996. First, it was an online e-Zine (a term that came and went with the Information Superhighway), whose name I can't remember. I assure you nobody else can recall the name either.

Then it was PC World magazine, and South Florida's Daily Business Review. Finally, the Miami Herald.

This book is a collection of many of my columns through the years. What it offers you is a chance to learn a lot of stuff about a lot of things having to do with tech law. For depth, you'll have to hit the law reviews and textbooks. This is not a dry text.

This book, like my columns, is meant to be approachable and readable. If you're a businessperson who wants a good overview of tech law, this book is for you. If you're a law student considering a specialty in tech law, this will give you an easy reading overview of the trenches and what we really do as tech lawyers. If you're a lawyer and your idea of contact with the Net is watching your kids Instant Message their friends, this book will help you learn to spot the issues and give you a glimpse at the answers. Whoever you are, this book will give you an excellent overview of the field.

I want to thank my wife Margie for encouraging me to write and understanding when I wasn't available because of it. I want to thank my three kids, Lisa, Jon, and Jessy, for being quieter on Saturdays because Dad was writing.

I would like to acknowledge Allison Hift, Bradley Gross, and Brian Nelson for contributing material.

If it weren't for the proofreading abilities of my long-time assistant, Patricia Kemp, my newspaper editors would have had more work. She probably has the distinction of being the only person, other than me, who has read every single column I've written. And she survived.

Jill Weiss, an instructor at Florida International University and teacher of courses like "Professional Ethics and Social Issues in Computer Science," was my one volunteer to read the entire manuscript and provide comments. I cannot thank Jill enough.

Finally, I want to thank my law clerks. They make me feel like a college football coach. Just when I fully train them, they graduate. I've had some excellent help over the years—Adam Feinsilver, Patricia Echeverri, Steve Canter, Tate Stickles, Sarah Santoro, and many others.

I would love to hear your comments about this collection. As I sit here, in 2003, I have to consider what my "permanent" e-mail address will be. I mean, if you buy this book at an estate sale in 2023, I especially want to hear from you. So, I'm guessing my permanent address will be MarkG@MGrossman Law.com. Please let me know your thoughts about this book.

Chapter One

The Law: Technology, Copyright, and Intellectual Property

WHAT IS TECHNOLOGY LAW?

I started describing myself as a lawyer with a practice that focused on "computer and tech law" over 14 years ago. When I'd tell people this, they'd look at me somewhat quizzically. You know—the same look you would expect if you'd just told them that E.T. was in your yard.

After that "look" went away, they would typically ask me two questions. What exactly is a "computer lawyer" and can you make money doing it?

As for the second question, nobody ever asks me that anymore. A decade ago, I'd say, "Sure you can. Really! Don't look at me that way. You can!"

At least I hoped so.

What's in a Name?

A lot's changed in 14 years. In that time, I've watched this area go through many incarnations even in its names.

The list is long and includes Internet law, e-commerce law, cyberlaw, and tech law. The names reflect the evolution of what was hot in the area.

To some extent, we still use all these names. The only one that hasn't aged well is "cyberlaw."

A few years ago, "cyberlaw" sounded right. Today, it sounds "old-fashioned" like the "Information Superhighway" (where did it go?) and the word "groovy." ("Groovy" may have been a kewl word when you were a kid, but today, saying it is a sure way to get that "You're a 'dork' look" from your kids—and your friends too.)

A decade ago, a computer lawyer did things like contracting for custom software development, intellectual property (heavy on the copyright side and light on the patent side) for software, and technology related litigation.

While any good litigator can handle the "network is dead" lawsuit, it takes a bit more finesse and knowledge to handle the "network is slow," "the software crashes too often," or "the system is not performing to our expectations." One of the problems with tech litigation is that you have to litigate these mushy issues all too often.

The specialty developed (the Florida Bar doesn't yet technically recognize it as a specialty) because people were spending big money on technology and the typical lawyer in 1990 viewed the computer as the $3000 typewriter on his secretary's desk.

One of the results of most lawyers being technologically challenged was that they were completely unprepared to deal with the contracting and litigation that arose from tech deals. You can't even ask the right questions if you're clueless.

Tech law, or whatever you want to call it, has exploded in the last five years. It reflects the way technology and particularly the Internet have entered our lives.

It really wasn't that long ago that TV commercials and billboards weren't obliged to send you to www.OurWebsite.com.

What Tech Law Has Become

Tech law today is still about the same things I did more than a decade ago, but now it's so much more. New issues seem to arise everyday and inevitably it takes awhile for the answer to evolve.

What's scary about this process of legislating is that the Internet and technology have brought many fundamental changes to our society and, in many cases, the people legislating know so little about the e-world. I have a problem with Internet related legislation being influenced by a guy who thinks that surfing the Web means watching his grandkids play on AOL.

E-Commerce Law

The hot issues evolve, but today include e-commerce and privacy.

As e-commerce grows, businesses want to decrease their reliance on paper and old ways of doing business. The problem is that the law has been playing catch-up.

For example, businesses have clamored for years for assurances that a contract "signed" electronically was as real and enforceable as a traditional paper contract. All too often, tech lawyers haven't been able to provide that complete assurance because the law was unclear and undeveloped. Now this area is getting legislative attention.

Privacy Online

Real people want to know what happens to the digital data they provide to websites. They offer some of it voluntarily by answering questions like name and address. Some websites collect information, like "clickstream" data, without the surfer's knowledge.

"Clickstream" is a type of information collection that makes some people uncomfortable. Literally, it's a record of your clicks. It may tell a website things like from what website you came, what you clicked on while in their website, and what website you went to after leaving their site.

Is this an invasion of privacy? Should the collection of this data be disclosed? These are some of the hot and heavy issues we'll see legislation addressing in the near future.

Businesses ask tech lawyers things like what data they can collect, what can they do with it once they have it, and what must their privacy policy say? In many cases, the answers from even a year or two ago are wrong today. That's how fast things are changing.

So, what's tech law? It's a legal area that's developed because of the new and unique legal issues that arise from the use of computers and other technology.

It's a multi-disciplinary area that encompasses things like contract, tort, copyright, employment, trademark, constitutional, banking, and criminal law. In some ways, it's a narrow area in that it deals with only technology-related issues. In other ways, it requires a lawyer to be a jack of all trades.

FIRST AMENDMENT AND
INTERNET BROADCAST

Have you heard the one about the company that wants to broadcast Timothy McVeigh's execution over the Internet? If it sounds to you like a perverse and surreal joke, the problem is that it isn't. If you want to know the name of the company, you're not going to find it here. Its obscene publicity stunt isn't going to get its name in print here. I'll just call it the "webcaster."

In its motion to the court, the webcaster said that, "The people of the United States, as citizens and as victims of the bombing, have a right pursuant to the First Amendment of the United States Constitution to oversee the implementation of justice against Mr. McVeigh, namely, to witness his execution." Wow—can you imagine that the webcaster filed this lawsuit to pro-tect our First Amendment rights?

Now, if this scenario hasn't yet struck you as truly surreal, let's add one more fact. Some of the more vocal advocates for the webcaster are those who are opposed to the death penalty. Their thing is that people will find the implementation of the death penalty so distasteful that they'll demand that the government abolish it.

This strikes me as perverse in the same way that anti-abortionists killing doctors and environmentalists acting like terrorists does. I suspect that most people who oppose the death penalty or are against abortion or consider themselves to be environmentalists cringe when they're associated in the same breath with those who are willing to go so over the line to advocate their positions.

Amendment Limits

Let's start by identifying my bias. I'm a huge advocate for the First Amend-ment. The thought of the government censoring the press, the Internet, or a book publisher makes me cringe.

I'm prepared to allow Nazi animals to march in Times Square because of my First Amendment principles. I'm prepared to tolerate flag burning although I think it's deplorable conduct.

I don't think that it follows that in the name of the First Amendment we have to revert to executions being performed in a circus-like atmosphere. And if you don't think the presence of a camera can't change the atmosphere of an otherwise solemn place, I think that you only need to remember the OJ trial to recall how even a murder trial could become a circus.

Even the First Amendment has limits. It's a cliché that you can't yell "fire" in a crowded theater. We all know that it's illegal to incite a riot.

In 1890, the United States Supreme Court upheld a state's total ban on both media and public access to executions. The Court held that "[t]hese are regulations which the legislature, in its wisdom, and for the public good, could legally prescribe in respect to executions occurring after the passage of the act."

Courts have never construed the First Amendment as an absolute grant of authority for the press to go everywhere and report everything.

In a 1996 case, a United States Court of Appeal ruled that the First Amend-ment didn't prohibit a Pentagon policy allowing the families of soldiers killed abroad to prevent the press from attending the return of the bodies to Ameri-can soil. In its opinion, the court said that "First Amendment rights to 'free-dom of speech, [and] of the press' do not create any per se right of access to government property or activities simply because such access might lead to more thorough or better reporting."

In 1980, the Supreme Court upheld denying a press request to visit a jail for reporting on jail conditions. The Court noted that it had "never intimated a First Amendment guarantee of a right of access to all sources of information with government control." Further, it said that the "undoubted right to gather news—affords no basis for the claim that the First Amendment compels others—private persons or governments—to supply information."

We shouldn't allow the First Amendment to be used as a weapon by those who want to appeal to the lowest element of our society. I can't imagine that the webcaster's motives are the noble protection of our First Amendment. Who are they kidding? If for a second you believe that, please look in the mirror. I suspect that you have a neon sign flashing on you head blinking, "Gullible fool."

Hey, if we're going to webcast this thing, let's do it right. Let's get it on the big screen in Times Square. Let's have that image of hundreds of thousands of Americans chanting, "Kill him" beamed around the world. Now, that would be something to be behold.

The government's rules prohibiting the broadcasting of the execution don't prevent reporting of or commentary on the event. That would trounce on the First Amendment. We're not even dealing with a total ban of the press or public, which the Supreme Court has previously blessed.

When McVeigh died, representatives of the press and the public, and victims' families attended. The event was widely reported, commented upon, and dominated the news for days.

The First Amendment doesn't require us to broadcast this ugly and horrific image. The First Amendment doesn't exist so that we're forced to give in to the most undignified and uncivilized elements in our society. At its most basic level, it exists to ensure unlimited political commentary, unfettered by government interference, that we had before, during and after this execution, whether we broadcast it live to appease the lynch mob or not.

COPYRIGHT LAWS ON THE INTERNET

Why is it that intelligent and well-educated people believe that copyright law doesn't apply to the Net? It might be because copying is so easy to do. Maybe it goes back to the almost utopian and non-commercial origins of the Net. Whatever the reason, it's a myth.

The simple fact is that copyright law applies as much to material posted on a website as it does to material printed in a book. It's not necessarily okay to save a picture from somebody's website and reuse it on your website.

Copyright law gives a copyright owner the right to control things like selling, renting, leasing, public performance and display, or lending of copies of copyrighted material. While the law protects a creator's expression of ideas, it doesn't protect the idea itself. Therefore, it's not an infringement to read an idea expressed by an author and then write about it in your own words.

This distinction between the expression of an idea being protected but not the idea is an example of how you can effectively and legally work with copyrighted material without infringing on the copyright owner's rights. Another example is the concept of "fair use."

"Fair use" is the way the law tries to balance the "needs of the one against the needs of the many." (You Trekkers know that I borrowed this last phrase, but I think it was a "fair use.") The public interest favors the wide dissemination of information while the copyright owner's interest favors royalties in his pocket if somebody uses his material. The law has to do what it often does: balance two competing interests.

"Fair use" allows copying "for purposes such as criticism, comment, news reporting, teaching (including multiple copies for classroom use), scholarship, or research . . ."

The problem with relying on "fair use" as the basis for your use of copyrighted materials is that you can rarely be positive that if tested in a courtroom, that your use would ultimately be found to be a fair use. A "fair use" determination requires you to look at four statutorily required factors and then judge how the answers should be determined in your case. The penalty for an incorrect judgment is that you'll be dubbed an infringer.

The first factor is "the purpose and character of the use, including whether such use is of a commercial nature or is for nonprofit educational purposes."

In analyzing this first one, you need to look at a few things. You start with the issue of whether it's a commercial use or a nonprofit educational use, with educational uses getting more leeway. Still, don't make the mistake of thinking that schools can do whatever they want with copyrighted materials. Schools have limits too or they wouldn't pay for textbooks (and nobody would have the incentive to write them.)

If it's not a nonprofit educational use, you look to see whether the use is for things like criticism, comment, news reporting, or research. These are other examples of uses that a court is more likely to find to be a fair use.

Finally, in analyzing the first factor, you need to look at the degree that you've changed the original. The more different it is than the original, the better.

The second statutory factor is "the nature of the copyrighted work." This factor acknowledges that not all copyrighted works were created equal. For example, the law views this area differently than a movie script. It tolerates copying facts more than it does copying a creative writing work.

The third factor is "the amount and substantiality of the portion used in relation to the copyrighted work as a whole." So, if you copy a full page from a four-page website, that looks like an infringement. If you take that single page from an online encyclopedia, it's probably "fair use." (Of course, passing it off as your writing might be unethical plagiarism, but that doesn't necessarily make it illegal.)

There is no clear ration test here. It's conceivable that using an entire original work could be fair use, while for something else, under different circumstances, using even a small part of the original might be an infringement.

The fourth and final factor is "the effect of the use upon the potential market value or value of the copyrighted work." So, if you copy an entire article from CNN's website, you may be a copyright infringer since you've arguably reduced the market for their site. The recipient of your copy has no need to visit CNN's site. You gave them the article.

If you were to copy the headline and first paragraph, and then told them to go to CNN.com for the rest, you're more likely to have the protection of "fair use." If anything, you've helped create a potential market by giving a teaser sample of the whole article.

The upshot of this brief foray into "fair use" is that when in doubt, ask the copyright owner's permission. "Fair use" is often the answer to why it's okay to quote or copy copyrighted material, but still there is nothing safer than asking permission.

COPYRIGHTS IN CYBERSPACE: DIGITAL LAWS AND THE INTERNET

On Oct. 28, 1998, then-President Clinton signed the Digital Millennium Copyright Act (DMCA) into law. Think of it as the Federal government's first shot over the bow at dealing with the many intellectual property issues raised by our new digital world.

In theory, the Internet could be the perfect way to bring information into homes and businesses. No more runs to the library to borrow a book or the store to buy a CD. The problem with translating the theory to reality is that this new digital medium raises many troubling and fundamental questions that remain largely unanswered. For example, should we allow libraries to "loan" a digital copy of a book and do we want Napster to make music freely available on the Net?

The simple reality is that the Net is still pretty new. This thing that comes into millions of our homes with websites, music, entertainment, chat, information, e-commerce and the list goes on endlessly, may feel like it's been around a long time, but it hasn't.

Just five years ago, it would have been fair to describe the entire body of Internet law as a pamphlet. Now, we're up to a few volumes, but it's going to take many more years for it to develop to the point where the law answers even fundamental Internet law questions. In 1998, Congress took a shot at adding to a sparse body of law.

The DMCA does things like make it illegal to "manufacture, import, offer to the public, provide, otherwise traffic in (sounds like we're dealing with illegal narcotics here) any technology, product, service, device, component—that is primarily designed or produced for the purpose of circumventing a technological measure that effectively controls access to a [copyrighted] work."

In plain English, the DMCA makes it illegal to circumvent copyright protections built into software to prevent piracy, and also prohibits the manufacture, sale, or distribution of code-cracking devices used to unlawfully copy software.

There are some exceptions to these prohibitions. For example, you can circumvent copyright protection devices to conduct encryption research and test computer security systems. Also, nonprofit libraries, archives, and educational institutions get their own limited exceptions.

If you're getting the feeling that this is a complex and detailed statute, you're right. But look at what Congress had to tackle. The issues are intrinsically complex, inherently new, and you have competing and divergent interests everywhere.

Libraries want to loan and archive literary works. Publishers want to sell them. Record companies want to package CDs with groups of songs. Web surfers want to download (and pay for?) only the songs they want. No more flip side of that 45 that nobody listened to anyway.

Then you have Internet service providers and issues that they raise. For example, let's say you own a sports-oriented website where you have chat rooms, bulletin boards where people can post materials, and you do other things that create a sense of community among your users. What happens when one of your users posts a copyrighted photo of a baseball game?

In similar situations, copyright owners have sued website owners for copyright infringement. Basically, their claim is that since it's your website, you're responsible for the infringement. The problem for the website owner is that she has no practical way to control all the zeros and ones flowing upstream and downstream to and from her site.

DMCA took a stab at creating an equitable solution for all those concerned by limiting the liability of ISPs if they do what the DMCA requires. If you let people post to your website and you haven't complied with the DMCA, then this is your wake-up call. This should be a major priority for you. After all, it's not often that Congress gives you a checklist of things to do to protect yourself from liability.

It starts by you designating an agent to receive notices of alleged copyright infringement. You should send the name and address of this agent to the Copyright Office and post the information on your site.

Next, you should have your tech lawyer develop a policy for dealing with alleged infringement. It should include a policy for terminating repeat offenders. You should post this policy on your website.

Then you'll want to set up an internal group to deal with complaints about alleged infringement. The DMCA requires you to "respond expeditiously to remove, or disable access to, the material that is claimed to be infringing."

The DMCA then gives an ISP a safe haven by providing that an ISP isn't liable for taking down any material if it believes in good faith that it is a copyright infringement. This is true even if a court ultimately decides that it wasn't an infringement.

While the DMCA created as many questions as it answered, I've got to give Congress and the Clinton administration credit for taking a good first shot at some difficult and controversial issues.

DIGITAL BROADCAST FLAGS

With the advent of digital data (you know, the zeros and ones), we have essentially perfected the ability to make copies. The days when each copy of a copy was worse than the copy before are now over. They're all perfect. This fact makes Hollywood and the music industry crazy. Remember Napster (may it rest in peace)?

The problem is that perfect copies are just too easy to make. To content providers like moviemakers, this could mean that if they broadcast a movie over digital television (coming to your family room soon), and you record it using your DVD-RW (devices that allow you to record onto a DVD), you can have it forever without paying them for that right. And, if that's not bad enough (let's face it, you can already do that with your VCR), you can then post it on the Net for others to copy.

The industries with the most money to lose here, like the movie and record industries and television broadcasters, would like to adopt copy protection schemes that prevent or at least "inhibit" people from making improper copies of the content that they invested money to provide. In their perfect world, they would have the government require that hardware devices used to play the content, like digital televisions, implement, rather than thwart, the copy protection scheme embedded in the digital content.

I do emphasize the word "inhibit" because let's not forget one of the axioms of any defensive tactic. For every measure, there's a countermeasure and for every countermeasure, there's a counter-countermeasure, and so on. So, while no measure is likely to keep the devoted hacker out for long, it may keep Joe Websurfer out.

Broadcast Flag

One of the controversies brewing now has to do with what's called a "broadcast flag." Essentially, a "broadcast flag" is a string of digital code that broadcasters would embed in a digital TV broadcast. Its purpose would be to tell your DVD player and PC that you're not authorized to retransmit this content over the Net.

The industries that are pushing for a legislatively mandated digital flag say that it won't stifle innovation. Rather, they insist that it will enable content providers to release more of their programming in a digital format and thus give us all more options.

So, who's opposed? It's the usual suspects like the Electronic Frontier Foundation (eff.org) and the Center for Democracy and Technology (cdt.org). According to the EFF, "Whatever measures the studios take to 'protect' their product from their customers will have to be applied to PCs too. The tamper-resistant seal around their devices will have to be wrapped around your software and hardware." So?

I'm sorry, but while I like free stuff as much as the next guy and though I may have more than just looked at Napster, I think it's time for some maturity to set in here. By "maturity," I mean that we come to accept that the hippy-commune-build-computers-in-your-garage-share-software-share-everything-days are over. Man, you can get viruses that way.

I'm so tired of the whining by the utopians who think this life is one big commune. Folks—content costs lots of money to create. It's also private property. Like any other private property, people and corporations (yes, my utopian friends, even those evil corporations) are entitled to take reasonable measures to protect their right to control their private property. If they can't protect it, they won't create it. If they do create it, they're only going to distribute it in ways that they can reasonably protect and police.

While your utopia may be a world filled with easily copied bootlegged content, mine is a world where I pay a fair price to enjoy content. You may like searching poorly constructed websites looking for good copies that download unpredictably and slowly. I don't have the time or the patience for that and at a higher level—it's stealing. And you know it.

We live in a world where pretty much all content could live on the Net, be available to your PC, and you would never have to leave your house or office. It "could" because those who create and own content often won't put it on the Net because they don't believe it's safe there, and in many ways they're right. The temptation to copy and redistribute is just too great and this is inhibiting the growth and development of the Net.

I think that it's time that we accept that broadcast flags and other copy protection schemes will be a part of our lives. It's really no different from a fence around your house. It's your property marker; it's your message to the world that this is yours and digital content is really no different. For you utopians out there, you're just going to have to accept that if there is no profit in content because people steal it, there won't be content.

INTELLECTUAL PROPERTY
DUE DILIGENCE

Intellectual property may be among the most valuable assets your company owns. The problem with intellectual property (IP) is that by its nature it's intangible. You can't touch it or see it. So how do you know what you have and own?

The starting point is to look to any registrations you may have with the government. For example, you may have registered a copyright or trademark and have paperwork to prove it. However, the registrations are just the starting point. It turns out that getting a handle on your company's IP assets can be a complex process.

Why Bother?

Great—so far I've told you that it's complex and we both know that you have a business to run and a to-do list that's a mile long. So, why would you ever take on this project?

Sometimes outsiders force you to dig into your IP assets as a part of their due diligence on your company. This could come up if somebody is buying shares in your company or acquiring some of your IP assets. A bank may require due diligence on your IP before it accepts IP as collateral.

I advise my clients to allow us to do an IP audit for them before anybody asks. This type of self-audit prepares companies for externally conducted due diligence and can enhance their own IP planning and management.

The first time a lawyer audits your IP, it can be time consuming. Usually, I've found that the record keeping is less than pristine and that basic questions lead to lots of head scratching. The time to deal with these issues and get your IP portfolio in order isn't when you need a loan secured by your IP or you have an investor with a pocket full of money who wants a full accounting of your IP assets. The time to do it is now without a deadline hanging over anyone's head.

Bear in mind that the nature of IP audits is that it's often an on and off process that can go on for weeks. This is unavoidable when you need documents from the government or, as is sometimes the case, signatures on agreements to clean up problems that your lawyer finds. The process can seem glacially and unacceptably slow if you need that money, but it all hinges on completing the IP audit.

What You Will Learn from an Audit

A properly conducted IP audit will analyze a textbook set of questions. The most basic is whether your company owns the rights. If your reaction is, "Of course we own it," guess what, maybe not. There are more ways to screw up ownership to IP than you can imagine.

For example, have you ever hired an independent contractor to create IP for you? It might have been a company to develop your website, an advertising agency to develop your ad campaign or whatever. In a great example of one of many ways to screw up in the world of IP is that if you don't have a written agreement that clearly and properly says that you own the IP, then your independent contractor owns it although you paid for it. Ouch.

I'd hate to be you when you're explaining to your board how you spent $100,000 on a website and don't own the copyright. Maybe somebody can get Paul Simon to write a song called, "A Hundred Ways to Lose Your IP."

Then if you own it, the next issue is have you adequately protected it? A part of the audit will also look at whether your right to use the IP is dependant on rights from a third party. For example, you may have custom created software modules that you own, but you may not be able to use them without a license to some underlying software.

Another issue that your audit will explore is whether the scope of your rights is sufficient for you to exploit your IP. Moreover, it you have exploited your rights, have you done so properly? This will look at issues like whether you've kept control of your IP through proper license and confidentiality agreements. A case in point would be letting third parties use your trademark without any controls in place. This could cause you to lose a trademark even if you registered it.

The final question I like to answer in my IP audits is whether the IP rights you're asserting present a risk of litigation. Here, I'll deal with issues like, does anyone else claim overlapping rights?

My suggestion is that you not wait for some third party to force you to get your arms around your IP assets. You should want to do it for your benefit. You need to know what you have, and if there are problems with what you think you have, it's better to deal with it sooner instead of later.

PROTECT YOUR SOURCE CODE

Whenever your business makes a significant investment in a software license, you have to consider the question, what if the developer goes out of business or refuses to properly support the software? Imagine a million dollar investment in software and then your developer goes under. How would you maintain the software without them? Could you add features as needed? Could you continue to upgrade your million dollar investment to keep up with the latest and greatest?

The starting point in answering these questions is for you to understand what it is you licensed. Generally, when you license software, you receive the object code. In plain English, "object code" is code that only your computer can read. Mere humans don't program using object code.

Humans write programs using what's called "source code." "Source code" is simply human-readable code. Generally, you can't do anything about rewriting software code unless you have the source code. Therefore, if your developer goes bankrupt and you don't have the source code, it would be fair to say you have a disaster in the making.

This problem isn't easily resolved because developers generally won't give you their source code because it's their ultimate trade secret. With the source code, a competitor could steal their work and build on it.

The generally accepted solution is that you and your software developer agree to place the source code in escrow with a trusted third party like DSI Technology Escrow Services (www.dsiescrow.com). The deal is essentially that you don't see or have access to the source code unless certain release conditions occur. Typically, these release conditions include things like the developer's bankruptcy or failure to provide support as required by your agreement with them.

There are many factors that you and your technology lawyer need to consider in deciding whether you should escrow your source code. While having that discussion, you also need to consider what type of verification you'll do if you escrow the source code.

"Verification" is something you need to consider because a CD, which is purported to have the source code for your software, is not something you can hold up to the light, like your parent's old Super 8 movies, and say, "Yup, it's the source code."

The fact is that when your escrow company receives what it thinks is the source code, it has no way of knowing what's on the media (like a CD) without going through some kind of verification process. Typically, verification is an additional service escrow companies would like to sell you—and that you should buy.

Could you imagine this scenario? You choose the vendor. Your company invests lots of money in licensing software from them based on your decision. Then, the company goes into bankruptcy. Your personal stock in the company is losing value because, "You chose them and it's your fault."

Ah, but you have your ace in the hole. You escrowed the source code!

So now, you request a release from escrow. You receive your source code. You stick the disk in your CD drive and you find Bugs Bunny cartoons playing on your computer where source code should be. Oops. At this point, I'm glad I'm not you and I'd suggest that you dust off that resume.

The point is that you have no way of knowing what's on that disk without verification. My take on verification is that it's not worth doing an escrow without at least some minimal form of verification.

According to John Boruvka, Vice-President and General Manager of DSI Technology Escrow Services, "About 80% of verifications fail."

Think about that statistic for a moment. It means that you only have a one in five chance of your escrowed source code working right when and if you need it. Precisely why you need to verify!

Verification is a time consuming process that will cost several thousand dollars at a minimum. Your actual cost will vary depending on things like the complexity of the software and the degree of verification you want.

Most escrow companies offer varying levels of verification with increasing cost. A basic verification might include things like confirming the program content, reading the media, identification of third-party libraries, and virus scanning.

At its most intense level, verification is a series of tests on your premises that validates that the source code is actually the source code for the software you use and that you have everything you need to deal with a disaster like your developer's bankruptcy. Here, your costs escalate because of the labor-intensive nature of this process.

There is no single right answer to the question, what level of verification do you need. It's a complex cost-benefit analysis that you must undertake with your IT folks, key end-users within your organization, and your tech lawyer.

While an escrow and expensive verification may not be the correct decision every time, not properly walking through the cost-benefit analysis is always the wrong answer.

SOURCE CODE ESCROW

Here's a nightmare you'll wish would end with you waking up. Your company spends $500,000 to license some software. Then the company you paid half a million dollars to goes bankrupt. Now you have $500,000 worth of orphaned software. I'll take a rain check on being you while you're explaining this one to the board.

Here's the problem in a nutshell. When you license software, you typically get a license to use what's called the "object code." Object code is the machine-readable code. Not even the nerdiest computer nerd you know can read object code.

Mere humans read and work in source code. Source code is simply computer code humans can read.

If your software developer goes under or can't support you, you'll need the source code if you're going to have any hope of hiring your own programmer to fix bugs, develop new features, or make any changes in the computer code you're using.

Here's the rub. You want to have the source code in case you need it. Your developer doesn't want to give it to you because they consider it their ultimate trade secret. The problem is that from their perspective they're right.

Developers never want to give you the source code because it's their life-blood. It's the secret sauce that prevents you from easily stealing their intellectual property.

The compromise is a source code escrow.

The typical setup will have the developer deposit the source code in escrow with a trusted third party. The escrow agreement requires the escrow agent to not release the source code to you unless certain release conditions are met. These conditions will typically be things like the developer's bankruptcy or failure to support you as required by your agreement.

While the basic outline of a software escrow may sound simple, it turns out that these are relatively complex deals. Many of the companies that handle escrows have model agreements on the Web, which make for a good starting point and certainly an improvement on reinventing the wheel. But the key word is "model" agreement.

Every deal is different. There are traps for the unwary and inexperienced throughout the process.

As you delve into this area, you'll find that many areas of the law are implicated, including bankruptcy and intellectual property law. Do it wrong and a bankruptcy court may prevent the release from escrow although you have an agreement that would appear to require it. Screw up on the intellectual property side and you may find out that you don't have the license you need to do what you thought you could with the source code.

Here are three quick tips on doing this right:

Make sure that your agreement requires them to promptly deposit revised source code once they release a new version.

When you negotiate for this requirement, don't do what almost everybody does in this situation, which is, of course, forget about it. You have to ensure that somebody in your organization is responsible for monitoring these future deposits. If you don't, my experience tells me that the developer will usually forget to make the deposits.

Verify that they've escrowed everything that is supposed to be escrowed and that the CD-ROM or other media is holding what it purports to be holding.

To verify, you'll need to have an agreement with your developer to have a trusted third party work with the source code to confirm that it is what it purports to be and that it's complete. The problem with verification is that it can be expensive.

The last cautionary word is to avoid the developer's already established escrow setup. Every arrangement I've ever seen like this has an escrow agreement in place that's extremely one-sided in favor of the vendor.

TRADEMARK LAW OVERVIEW

As a tech lawyer, my clients frequently have questions about trademark law. Whether it's because they're launching a new venture online or because they realize that exposing their trademark to the world on the Net means that their trademark may get more scrutiny from competitors and others, they ask lots of questions. My goal here is to provide you with a businessperson's overview of trademark law.

Let's start with a working definition. A "trademark" is any work, name, symbol, or device, or combination of these that you might use to identify and distinguish your goods for those manufactured or sold by others. Trademarks refer to goods. Technically, if you're referring to services, it's not a trademark, but rather a "service mark." Many people use "trademark" to loosely include "service mark" although that is not technically correct. At the risk of causing a professor of intellectual property to lose a night's sleep (can they revoke my law degree?), I'm going to use "trademark" to include "service mark."

Choose carefully. While even simple dictionary words like "Apple," as in the computer company, can be trademarks, it's important to understand that not all trademarks are created equal. There is a continuum of strength for trademarks. You want to be thoughtful about the trademark you choose so that yours is a stronger one.

The strongest trademarks are "arbitrary" or "fanciful" ones. An "arbitrary" trademark is one that doesn't even suggest the goods or services you're labeling. A "fanciful" trademark consists of a word you make up to apply to goods or services.

Classic examples of arbitrary trademarks are "Apple" for computers and "BlackBerry" for those handheld e-mail devices. Other good examples of fanciful trademarks include "Xerox," "Ketchup," and "Lucent." These are powerful and easy to enforce trademarks. They were not in the dictionary when created and if you try to use a word that's even close, you may find yourself at the wrong end of a Federal judge's ire.

Next down in strength are "suggestive" trademarks. These indirectly describe or "suggest" whatever it is they identify. "LinkSys" is a good example of a suggestive trademark. It's a brand for networking equipment that "links your system" together. Cute—and it's a relatively strong trademark.

Next down in the continuum of strength are "descriptive" marks. These marks describe the goods or services. An example would be "The Weather Channel." Descriptive marks are not registrable as trademarks until they develop what's called a "secondary meaning." What that means is that you're going to have to prove that people really think of your product or service in connection with the mark. That's not easy.

The weakest kind of mark and one not entitled to registration as a mark are "generic" marks. Sorry, but you can't register "personal computer" or "television" to describe a personal computer or television.

Think about registering your trademark. However, what's interesting about trademarks is that they arise from use, not government registration. If you make up a word and apply it to goods, you have a trademark. It's that easy.

While it is true that you aren't required to register a trademark with the government, it's still an excellent idea for many reasons. For one, registration is strong evidence that you in fact own the mark. It's also a truism that a registered mark is far more valuable than an unregistered mark. So, if you ever dream of selling your company or bringing in outside investors, they'll be favorably impressed if your registrations are in order.

Another reason is that in the online world, if you have to battle a cybersquatter for taking a domain name that is based on your trademark, you'll be in a much stronger position if your mark is registered.

One more example of an advantage of registration is that you are then entitled to use the symbol "®" in association with your mark. That little symbol sends a powerful message to would-be trademark infringers that you have a registered trademark and can invoke all of the remedies provided by federal trademark law.

If you choose not to register your trademarks (hold out your hand so I can slap your wrist), you still should tell the world that you claim a trademark, albeit an unregistered one. You do this by putting "tm" next to your trademark or "sm" next to your service mark. At the least, it takes away the "Gee wiz, I didn't know it was a trademark" defense. Moreover, in case you were wondering, "gee wiz" is a technical legal term, but that's for another chapter.

Bottom line business advice for the average businessperson concerning trademark law comes down to this: register your marks, and use a competent tech or intellectual property lawyer to handle it for you. Have no fear; your registration won't send a lawyer's kids through college because, in the grand scheme of things, a trademark registration is not expensive. Just budget for it and get it done—today. It's an essential investment in your business.

INVISIBLE TRADEMARKS?

Let's say you want to buy a Chevrolet. Looking for information, you go to your favorite search engine and type in "Chevrolet." If websites for other car brands popped to the top of your search results, you might wonder how that happened. The answer would probably be "metatags."

"Metatags" are words in a website that are hidden to the casual web surfer. You don't see the metatags because they're embedded in the hypertext markup language (HTML) code. ("HTML" is technospeak for the programming language used to create a website.) You can see the metatags if you choose "view" and then "source" from your browser's menu when you're at a website.

Metatags often include generic categories like "books," "computers," "legal services," or "doctor," but they can also include trademarked terms like "Addidas," "Quicken," "Xerox," or "Dell." Although you may not see the metatags, many search engines do and they use them to help the search engine rank results.

This means that if a website for another car brand includes the word "Chevrolet" in its metatags, when you search the word "Chevrolet," the website for this other brand will be included in the results generated by your search. Now if you're "Chevrolet," you might be less than pleased to find out that when people search for your brand, they get information about your competitors.

Clearly, you can't open a Ford dealership, put up a sign that says "Chevrolet," and then when a potential customer walks in trying to buy a Chevy, sell her a Ford. You don't need to go to law school to know that a "Chevrolet" sign in front of a Ford dealership is a trademark infringement.

Likewise, this hypothetical Ford dealer can't use the domain name "ChevroletInformation.com" to lure you to their site about Ford cars.

Again, common sense tells you that this would be over-the-line conduct and that this Ford dealer is going to end up on the wrong end of a Federal court lawsuit.

What both of these scenarios have in common is that the eyes of the most casual observer can see the word "Chevrolet" being used to sell Ford cars. What makes the metatag issue cute is that with metatags, the casual observer can't see that the Ford dealer's website is using the word "Chevrolet" to lure you to a Ford dealer's website.

So, can you infringe a trademark if the infringement is invisible? The question seems simple enough, but as with so many questions in Internet law, the answer isn't completely clear. The issue is just too new for our legal system to have formulated unambiguous answers.

What is clear is that this can be a treacherous area. The one thing that legal uncertainty generates is litigation as businesses look to courts to provide answers to confusing scenarios. Legal scholars and courts are grappling with this issue.

While traditional tests used to determine whether the particular use of trademarked terms is an infringement don't seem to perfectly fit the hidden metatag issue, I suspect that we'll see a trend where courts will be imaginative in stretching traditional doctrine to demonize metatags that use trademarks owned by others to draw traffic to a website.

After all, law should be about good public policy. From the consumer's perspective, it's a form of bait and switch to ask for information about Chevy and get Ford information instead.

Viewed another way—if the law is unclear, do you want to be the test case, which helps clarify the law for the benefit of others? Think about the potential number of zeros on the number when you consider a damage award against you if you lose, and the attorney's fees involved as you test the limits of the law.

Until the law is clearer, I recommend against using your competitors trademarks in your metatags. It's just begging for a problem.

If you hire an independent contractor website developer, I also recommend that you take control of the metatags. Most developers take the initiative with metatag creation and that's fine. In a way, part of what you're buying from them is their creativity in creating metatags for you.

Still, there may be legal consequences arising from the choice of metatags and you really should run the choice by your tech lawyer before your site goes live.

Now, there is a flip side to this too. Run your trademarks through all the search engines. You may just find that your competitors have used your trademarks to draw traffic to their site. If you discover that they have done this, I think that a cease and desist letter from your lawyer may be in order. If they won't back down, you have to evaluate whether you want to use your only sledgehammer—a lawsuit.

While expensive and a test case, I'd rather take this side of this test case because I think that most courts will see that good public policy requires the protection of trademarks even if the infringement is invisible to the casual eye.

Chapter Two

Venture Capital and Financiers: Getting Started Correctly

STARTING A BUSINESS

Once again, it's looking like a good time to start or grow Internet and tech businesses. My observation is that the CEOs, CFOs, CIOs, and other leadership of the last round of dotcom to dotbomb mania are back in high school. Now, it's safe for the rest of us to get going.

Having practiced law for more than 20 years and after doing this tech law thing for most of those years, I've seen my share of economic cycles. The list of tech products and businesses that have come and gone since the 70s is long and illustrious. Some disappeared, some merged into something else, and some are still around, but they may as well have disappeared.

Remember, "Central Point's PC Tools?" It used to compete with Norton Utilities. Do you remember "Zeos?" They sold mail order computers before Michael Dell was a household name.

We all watched the tech marketplace prove Newton right again as it fell precipitously. In the late 90s and into this new century, while the price for computer hardware dropped like a brick, the price for services rose to unaffordable levels.

Things changed quickly. In the mid 90s, web development was cheap because everyone was new at it and trying to develop a portfolio. In the late 90s, major web development could easily get you into the six and seven figures. Demand was high, skilled programmers were in short supply, and it was a seller's market.

For a while, it seemed that nobody but a dotcom could afford a Super Bowl commercial. Then, it all crashed and burned. At least, they didn't change the commercial to "BudBowl.com."

Now, I'm seeing a clear-up tick in the tech world. Interestingly, I started to see it in July and August of 2001, but then came 9/11. Everything seemed to stop for the balance of the year.

Now, I'm again seeing what I would characterize as a pleasingly surprising increase in tech activity. I'd divide it into several categories.

One kind is what I've come to call "salvage deals." The survivors of the tech sector's debacle started doing deals they couldn't possibly do at the top of the cycle. Often, they bought the tottering remains of startups from the mania period or jumped into deals where they replaced some failed tech company—but this time on business terms that made sense.

Website and software development has again become affordable. Guess what—the web developers and programmers who could command monstrous salaries in 1999 are simply looking for good work in 2003. The web project that was unaffordable in 1999 is suddenly affordable.

Economic reality hit the tech sector with the near collapse of the sector. It's been sobering, but undoubtedly a positive survival of the fittest experience.

The serial entrepreneurs who made some quick money early in the tech sector's rise to the stratosphere, but then may have made missteps later in the bubble period, are getting back in the game. People who had retrenched and seemed to almost disappear are calling me again.

Like a maturing child, I'm seeing some differences in the tech sector's business practices. Skateboards, Chief Morale Officers, pool tables, ginseng tea, and millions of dollars of funding based on 30-page business plans are definitely out. It's been some time since I saw a tech "contract" written on the back of a napkin. The "fun" part (lawyers do have a perverse sense of "fun") was litigating those napkins.

On this go around, "in" are Honda Civics, Chief Financial Officers, coffee, funding based on a functioning and profitable business, and contracts negotiated and drafted by skilled lawyers.

This time around, it's back to basics. There's less focus on "Internet speed" and more focus on "let's make sure that the two sides of the deal actually understand what each expects from the other before they begin the deal."

I'm no longer seeing business plans based on fantasy like 50% market share, and eight-figure revenue based on "first to market" and banner advertising revenue. Now, it's more like we have a functioning and profitable business, and we believe we can grow it faster if we do some key deals. Many of these involve brick and mortar businesses that now see a way to make the Net a profit center. It's now often clicks and mortar and variations on that theme.

Tech's been beaten up in the last couple of years, but it's not as if it's a passing fad. It's not going away. The sector is starting to churn again. Bargains abound in the marketplace and the next round of millionaires is ready to be made. It won't be the followers who get in at the new top. It will be the ones getting in now—at the new bottom—who use sound business practices to grow their tech business idea into something substantial. Now looks like the time to make your leap if you have dreams.

MONEY FOR STARTUPS: RAISING
VENTURE CAPITAL

If you want to turn your small e-business into a big e-business, you're going to need money, and lots of it. The big issue is how to find the money you'll need to get your e-business off the ground.

Just a year or two ago, venture capitalists (VCs) offered big money fast. These days, it's harder to get venture capital dollars.

Still, there's plenty of money floating around. However, in light of the recent spate of dotbomb deaths, VCs have become more selective in how and where they invest.

To attract venture capital dollars, you have to produce a viable business plan, a proven customer base, and a rudimentary revenue stream. In reality, most e-businesses that need money don't have these things.

Some e-businesses have found alternative sources of capital by offering equity investments to nontraditional sources of capital.

For example, competent legal counsel is something that e-businesses can't live without, but cash-poor startups often can't afford it. They often do their own legal work, and hope they can survive long enough to generate some funds.

Equity investments can change all this. Many cash-strapped e-businesses offer law firms stock in exchange for reduced-price services.

Like VCs, professionals are more reluctant to invest in startups than they were a year ago. Still, if you can find a willing professional, this could be a win-win situation.

If you're not quite ready to give up a piece of your company, Washington, D.C., has several bureaucracies that may be available to help finance your e-business.

One example is the Small Business Administration (SBA) [visit www.sba .gov/financing]. It offers commercial loans to e-businesses with terms more favorable than you'd find at most commercial banks. Further, the SBA licenses and regulates other private investment firms called SBICs (Small Business Investment Companies) [www.sba.gov/INV].

Of course, you'll first have to complete a lot of paperwork and then wait while your paperwork is processed.

Unfortunately, delays in closing loans can kill your e-business as thoroughly as if you had received no loan at all. Therefore, if you're thinking about applying for an SBA or SBIC loan, avoid putting all of your cash eggs in the same financing basket, and consider simultaneously pursuing other avenues of funding.

Founders of Internet startups often find it tempting to self-fund their companies. To do this, they often mortgage their family's home or withdraw their life savings.

I think this financing method is even scarier than watching your e-business go down the drain. After all, if you haven't invested all your personal funds in your e-business and your company fails, at least you have a place to call home. If you've leveraged your house to support your failed business, you may end up on the street.

Nonetheless, if you extend a personal loan to your e-business, remember that this should not be thought of as a "goal."

Instead, you should treat a personal loan as a "beginning," and use the money to support your company while seeking other sources of revenue. Once you secure those additional revenue sources, immediately pay back your personal loan.

Be aware if you find a VC: They don't like you paying yourself back with their money.

Finally, many businesses have started with funds from one of the three Fs of financing—friends, fools, and family. If you win your bet on your business, they win too.

With a bit of creativity, you can find revenue sources other than traditional venture capitalists. Speak to an attorney or accountant experienced in venture capital issues from the beginning. They're often plugged into a network of investors. Just a few minutes with a knowledgeable lawyer or accountant could save you hours of funding frustration.

BUSINESS PLANS

If you're seeking investors for your business, writing a business plan is one of those daunting tasks you'll have to face. Whether you choose to hire a professional business plan writer to help or you do it yourself, you'll need to be the chief architect of the ideas that will lead to success. Here are some tips to help you through the process.

Every plan should start with a one to two page Executive Summary. This section isn't a warm up, preface, forward, or "make 'em feel good (rah rah) about your business" section. Rather, it's your entire business plan reduced to its essence. And your essence had better boil because if it doesn't, they (the ones with the checkbooks) aren't going to read the rest of your plan.

Those of us who have to read business plans hate it. I've yet to meet anyone who would choose to read a business plan over doing—well anything else. It's amazing what it takes to make a dental appointment look like an attractive break.

Your Executive Summary must capture your reader. You have two pages to make your jaded reader want to learn more about you.

You have two pages to talk about things like your market, your product or service, why your management team is the best lineup put together since the squad that brought home Apollo 13, your projected revenues and expenses, how much money you're seeking, what you'll do with their money (this isn't the time to pay down the home equity loan) and, most importantly, "why you."

After the Executive Summary, I'm an advocate with front-loading your business plan with information about your management team. Tell the venture capitalist about the business experience and successes of the team.

It's a simple formula. VCs invest in people as much as, if not more than, they invest in technology. Most will tell you that they'd rather have an "A team" and a "B technology" than vice versa.

If there isn't much to say here, you're probably not going to find venture capital. You may not want to hear this, but the sooner you come to terms with this reality check, the sooner you can begin moving in a path that may lead to success—like adding strength to your management.

The next section begins the body of your plan. At some point, you're going to need to present the mundane facts. You'll talk about things like when you incorporated, who owns the company, and what you've accomplished.

Today, the venture capital market is clearly tighter than it was a year ago. More than ever, VCs are looking for new, unique, and hard to duplicate technologies and ideas.

The key to funding in today's market is a great explanation to answer what I referred to earlier as "why you." In writing your plan, never lose sight of the fact that VCs may read hundreds of business plans for every one they agree to fund.

People, like attorneys and accountants, who act as filters to VCs, similarly read many plans for every one they send to those in their venture capital network. Those of us who do this know that our credibility is at stake every time we forward a plan.

I know that if I want VCs to read the business plans I send, I have to prove to them that it only gets beyond me if it's quality. If any professional who gets involved in venture capital sends clunkers to VCs, he could find his packages heading straight for the trash.

Your plan must answer "why you" in such a way that it's clear that you have an unfair and sustainable advantage over your competition. You have to demonstrate how you'll survive direct competition, reverse engineering, and a bigger company entering your space. Further, you need to explain how you'll sustain any advantage you have.

Remember, VCs aren't looking for 10 or 15% per year return on their investment. They could invest in mutual funds and hope for that. They're looking for returns upwards of 25% per year and some would say upwards of 100% per year. Your plan must show that numbers like this are possible.

Now, of course, the paper will hold whatever numbers you put on it. While some level of optimism is acceptable in projecting your numbers, you should increase your anti-hallucinogenic medication to where your delusions are at a moderate level when you do the financial projections. Absurd projections won't help your cause.

If you want venture capital, hunker down and get to work on that business plan. When you have it done, don't mass mail it the VCs. Look to your network of professionals and friends to present it to a VC they know. Mass mailed business plans have something approaching zero chance of being funded—no matter how well written.

EXIT STRATEGIES

If you're with a technology company, you may be feeling the pain of the economic downturn more than most. While there are lots of lessons to glean from current events, one of the best is the importance of locating the exit door.

No, I'm not talking about the door that leads to the parking lot. Instead, I'm talking about the exit strategy that you should have included, but probably didn't, in all of your technology-based contracts. You probably didn't even realize you needed an exit strategy until your customers' wallets grew tight, your expenses began to pile up, and your contract obligations with your technology affiliates started to drain your company's operating account.

Let's go back a year or so ago. That was probably around the time you entered into that megamoney website development agreement. You had aspirations of building the perfect website. The website was going to knock the socks off your competition, and it was guaranteed to attract customers in droves.

Well, maybe it did, maybe it didn't. If it didn't, you found yourself in the same boat as dozens of other dotcoms: Bills were piling up but the customers weren't. When you went to cancel that costly website development contract, you might have come to some ugly realizations.

One might have been that you couldn't get out of the contract without shelling out big money to the developer. Another really ugly scenario might be that your developer—not you—owned the copyright to your website, and you weren't going to own it anytime soon without a costly legal battle. Last, but painfully not least, might be that you weren't quite sure whether the website would ever work again after the developer stopped supporting it.

The problem is, of course, that we don't like to think about the end of a contract. The end is depressing. Instead, we like to think about the money that we're going to make throughout the contract. Unfortunately, it's this type of thinking that will come back to bite you where you're most vulnerable.

Before we continue, keep this in mind: You shouldn't try to build or evaluate your exit strategy without help from your tech lawyer. This chapter isn't a legal textbook. There are too many contingencies that could arise in your contract, and I couldn't cover all of them even if I devoted 50 articles to the subject.

Five Points

That said, you should keep certain broad areas in mind when reviewing your exit strategy. Follow the oft-cited mantra of good reporting: Who, What, When, Where, and Why.

For example, consider who can terminate your contract. While no contract can legally bind you in such a way that you can never get out, you should never assume that you have the same rights to end the contract as the other party.

Second, think about what you have to do to end the contract. If you end the agreement after only a short time, will you have to pay out the remainder of the contract fees, or will you be liable only for those services that you have received up to the point of termination?

Third, consider how long it may take to cancel your obligations under the contract.

Fourth, think about where you would want to settle any dispute that might arise from your termination of the contract (read, "L-A-W-S-U-I-T").

Finally, think about all the situations in which you might reasonably want to cancel your contract, and make sure that your exit strategy covers you for all of those scenarios.

Chapter Three

Contracts and Contracting:
Laws, Issues, and Tips

WORKING WITH RFPS
(REQUESTS FOR PROPOSALS)

One of the time-tested ways of buying computer-related goods and services is to use a Request for Proposal (RFP). If your organization has never used an RFP before and you're considering a major investment in your computers or software, you should give some thought to an RFP.

An RFP is essentially a request for potential vendors to make offers to provide a service or product that matches your basic specifications and budget.

While I've helped create and have worked with RFPs that required loose-leaf binders, I've also helped to create some that are rather short. While governments may have requirements that lead to extremely formal and legalistic RFP processes, in the private world, you can create you own rules for the RFP process. You don't have to create a monster document, unless you choose to create a monster to suit your needs.

In fact, in the world of private industry, you can and should disengage yourself from the image you might have about government RFPs and their formalistic process. Hey, we get to make the rules.

If you don't want to be "required" to award the contract to the lowest bidder, then don't. We will just write the RFP in such a way that you have no such requirement.

If you want vendors to submit all their questions in writing with the question and answer going out to all bidders to keep the playing field level, then make that the rule. If you prefer to take informal phone calls or have a scheduled bidder's conference, then do that. The overriding point is that in private industry there is no right or wrong way to do an RFP. It's your game. You make the rules—subject to one important proviso.

As with everything else you do in business, you only have one reputation to go around. While I tell you that you can set the rules any way you want, I warn you that whatever rules you set, you should abide by them and not change them whimsically as the process progresses.

Conceivably, you could set yourself up for some kind of lawsuit if you play fast and loose with your own rules, but that's really not the big issue. You would almost have to work at it to end up on the wrong end of a lawsuit over an RFP. The real issue is your reputation.

The Basic Format

Experience has taught me that the time, money, and effort invested in writing an effective RFP on the front end can and will save you time, money, and effort at the back end of the contracting process. An RFP is an effective way for you to tell your vendor what it is you want and what you intend to invest to make it happen.

The most important component of an RFP is your detailed explanation of required functionality. You'll want to describe things like your operational requirements, performance standards, acceptance testing criteria, the operating environment including hardware, operating system and other software, your size and scalability requirements, delivery needs, and other related details.

Your tech lawyer should be sure that your RFP includes some basic protections for you. For example, you'll want it to be clear that the issuance of the RFP commits you to do nothing. You pay no costs associated with creating the response to the RFP, you don't have to enter into any contract with any of the potential vendors, and you won't provide any materials or labor.

From the Vendor's Perspective

While you don't want to ignore the rules your potential customer has created, you should construe every ambiguity in your favor to gain some advantage over your competitors. You need to use everything you know about your potential customer and read the RFP in context.

If you have contacts within your customer's organization, use them. An informal phone call handled properly might just give you the edge. Be careful here though. You don't want to cross any lines and do anything improper, but if you can, use your back channels to your advantage.

You might call your biggest fan in your customer's organization and ask if it's okay to discuss the RFP. Invite them to say "No." Often, when you're outside the realm of legalistic government contracting, you'll find that informal conversations may be welcome.

Once you get permission to start the conversation, ask away. Never lose sight of that cliché, "Information is power." The more you know about their wants, needs, expectations, predispositions, and whatever else it is that you can learn, the bigger the advantage you have over the competition.

Your response should get some level of legal review. As much as anything, the purpose of this legal review is to ensure that you haven't somehow created unintended legal obligations with your response. I can assure you that your customer has left themselves wiggle room for the final negotiation. You just want to be sure to do the same.

FORMING CONTRACTS ONLINE

When you've surfed the Web, you've probably noticed that some web pages have a link at the bottom of the page labeled something like "Terms and Conditions." If you've ever really been bored, you might have even clicked on the link to investigate. If you did, you probably found a contract that purported to govern your use of the site. Could a contract you didn't sign and that you didn't even have to read possibly be a real contract?

It turns out that this is actually an important and somewhat open question. It's important because if you own a website, the classic advice is that you must—absolutely must—have terms and conditions for website use. After all, it's your opportunity to have a completely one-sided agreement protecting your interests. However, how do you ensure that the contract you put on your site will hold up in court if you need it?

One-Sided

Let's start with the one-sided issue. Simply put, you can get away with one-sided because—well, let's face it—nobody reads these agreements.

So, when I write these agreements for clients, I like to include provisions like no warranties on uptime or the accuracy of the information presented. Another is that if you sue us, you have to do it in our local court, not yours. I'll also include a "Limitation of Liability," which when reduced to its essence says, "No matter what we do and no matter how bad it is, we owe you nothing or very little."

A Real Contract?

There are two common ways websites attempt to form contracts with users.

They are "clickwrap" and "browsewrap."

Clickwrap is when you're forced to affirmatively click on a button that says something like "I Accept" after you've been given the chance to read the Terms and Conditions of Website Use Agreement. If you don't click "I Accept," the website won't let you in.

You also see clickwrap when you install software. As you begin to install the software, a license pops up and you have to click "I Accept" before you can continue with the installation. Of course, you don't read it, print it, contemplate or think about it before you click "I Accept." (When they come to pick up your first born the next day, you might give some thought to that agreement you didn't read.)

Although even this point is not 100% clear, I think that it's fair to say that a clickwrap agreement is almost certainly a binding contract. Pretty much everything on the legal landscape is pointing toward validity and public policy would seem to favor their validity. If you're properly guided by your tech lawyer, you should be able to post a valid and enforceable agreement on your website.

The more problematic issue is "browsewrap." Courts seem less comfortable with the idea that an agreement "hidden" behind a little teeny tiny link at the bottom of a web page can be a binding contract.

In a case involving Netscape, the court took a negative view on browsewrap by saying that, "The case law on software licensing has not eroded the importance of assent in contract formation. Mutual assent is the bedrock of any agreement to which the law will give force."

Translated into English, the court said that you couldn't say that someone has agreed to something simply because there's a link at the bottom of a page inviting someone to read an agreement.

So, if clickwrap probably works and browsewrap is more problematical, why not just use clickwrap? I think that the answer lies in marketing and good business practices.

If you have a website that exposes your company to low legal risk, it would be a case of the "legal" tail wagging the "business" dog to inconvenience your website users with a clickwrap agreement. Legal considerations should not always override good business.

It's the nature of some websites that if you force users to go through a registration process and click "I Accept" before they can enter the site you will lose an unacceptable number of visitors. This is when you must consider using browsewrap rather than clickwrap.

Making Browsewrap Work

Although there is no certain way to ensure that a browsewrap will be enforceable if you ever need it in a courtroom, here are some ways to enhance the likelihood that you will be able to convince a court to enforce your browsewrap agreement.

First, make that "Terms and Conditions" link CONSPICUOUS and make it say "THESE TERMS AND CONDITIONS GOVERN YOUR USE OF THIS SITE. YOU MUST CLICK HERE BEFORE PROCEEDING."

If your site has multiple panes, you might consider putting this link in a persistent window that won't come and go as a surfer surfs.

In your agreement, be sure that you clearly state that by merely viewing your site, the web surfer agrees to be bound by this agreement.

If you take these steps, you're on the right path to enforceability.

LETTERS OF INTENT:
PROCEED WITH CAUTION

As a person who's always doing other people's tech deals, I understand and still get the adrenaline rush of closing the big deal. After almost two decades of practicing law, I'm still amazed at the number of legal fallacies that even sophisticated business people have about doing deals and properly documenting them. A prominent fallacy is that Letters of Intent (LOI) are always non-binding.

I suppose that the misconception arises because—well—it does say "Letter of Intent" and not "Contract" at the top of the page.

Do yourself a favor. Press the "I Believe" button on this one when I tell you that LOIs can be binding agreements—you need to take them seriously, and they need to be written by your attorney.

LOIs go by many names, such as Memorandum of Understanding, Agreement in Principle, and Term Sheet, among other things. Whatever you call them, they can bite you if you're not properly circumspect about the things you sign.

Yes, it's exciting when a venture capitalist wants to fund your tech company. (Yes, venture capitalists still fund tech companies.) I know that when they mention the LOI, it's a Right Guard moment. Just understand that once you sign that LOI, you may be blurring the line between engagement and marriage.

If you never close your deal because you never could work out all the details, you may find that LOI under lots of scrutiny. LOIs can and do end up in courtrooms. The essence of the lawsuit is often plain old "breach of contract."

It really comes down to this. Non-lawyers are often under the misconception that the title of the document absolutely governs the situation.

If the language in your LOI reads like a binding contract, it's probably a binding contract. Don't make the mistake of thinking that just because not every detail of your deal is in the LOI that this necessarily means you would win if sued.

The starting point in drafting an LOI is to remember its purpose. Usually, parties are looking to summarize their deal as a prelude to negotiating the details. It's usually intended to be superceded by a more formal and lengthy document.

Using a venture capital deal as the example, the LOI will deal with issues like the size of the investment, the type and quantity of stock that the venture capitalist will get, and other high-level issues. Usually, the parties don't intend for these terms to be binding if they never sign a more formal contract that includes all the details.

However, the parties usually have terms they do expect to be binding even if they never close the deal. Some examples would include a confidentiality provision and a provision that says each party is responsible for their own attorneys' fees and other expenses in connection with the negotiation of the deal.

If your LOI isn't specific about whether it's really a contract or a nonbinding summary of the state of your negotiations, you could be creating an unpredictable mess for yourself. If there's ever a dispute about the LOI, you're forcing a court to look at the document as a whole, accept testimony with those who participated in the LOI creation process, and then make an educated guess as to the intent of the parties.

In this situation, the fact that it says, "Letter of Intent" at the top is just a single piece of evidence that a court will use to find the parties' intent. If everything below the title reads like a binding agreement, the court may find that you have a contract, and not just the simple outline of terms to be negotiated that you thought you had.

In some ways, if your lawyer does it right, this can be simple. A well-drawn LOI has a provision that specifically states to what extent the parties intend it to be a binding agreement. A typical provision will say that the LOI in fact has provisions that the parties intend to be binding even if they never sign another document. It will then go on to specify those provisions.

Whatever you do, just remember that an LOI is a legal document, which you should have your lawyer write. If you think that you are up to the task, let me give you some perspective: As somebody who mentors young lawyers,

I've yet to find one who fell out of law school with an innate ability to draft legal documents. It takes years of mentoring and training for a young lawyer to master the art of legal writing. I just ask, "Who mentored you?"

NONDISCLOSURE AGREEMENTS: THE TRICKY ASPECTS

In the world of tech deals—more than other types of deals—my clients want to sign nondisclosure agreements (NDA) quickly. I'm sure that many people will disagree with me on this one, but I like to avoid NDAs in the early stages of a deal. My feeling is that you shouldn't be exchanging secrets with strangers, and that doesn't change no matter what they've signed.

Experience tells me that most deals at the "initial feeler" stage never reach fruition. It's a long way from that first lunch to a closing and a bottle of champagne. I say skip the paperwork and legal entanglements until you've at least gone as far as thinking: "This is getting interesting and serious." In the meantime, keep your secrets to yourself.

Usually, you can get through the early stages of a negotiation with a demonstration of what "it" can do without revealing how it does it. Of course, if what it does is as much a secret as how it does it, then my generalization may not be true for you.

In case you're not familiar with NDAs, the idea behind them is that you'll reveal confidential information only if the other side agrees not to improperly disclose or use the information. Right here it starts getting tricky because you have to decide to whom they can disclose it and for what use.

Watch out for a form with a line for your company name. If you're tempted to sign it, I have some simple advice: Don't. Not ever.

Every NDA is customized. Since tech lawyers see NDAs constantly, writing a good one should never be an exercise in reinventing the wheel. Still, they do require some thought.

For example, even the common name "Nondisclosure Agreement" is a bit deceptive because you not only want them to keep your secrets, you also don't want them to use them for their own benefit.

I'll typically include a provision like, "The company shall use the Secret Information only for the following purposes . . ." I'll then go on to list those purposes, which will vary in every deal, but never include exploiting my client's idea for their own benefit. So, it's not just "nondisclosure," it's also about not using my client's idea.

Make sure the agreement does a good job of distinguishing between confidential information and trade secrets. This is important because most NDAs have an expiration date after which a party is free to reveal the confidential information—and you never want that with a trade secret.

A trade secret is an idea that derives independent economic value from not being generally known or readily ascertainable by proper means by other persons who could obtain economic value from its disclosure. It must also be the subject of efforts to maintain its secrecy. One most famous example is Coca-Cola's secret ingredient.

While you could argue that the obligation to maintain confidentiality of your secrets should last forever, most people hate to have long-term agreements hanging out there. It's usually reasonable to compromise and come up with an expiration date when we're talking about confidential information that doesn't rise to the level of a trade secret.

Ironically, in the tech world, this expiration date usually doesn't need to be zillions of years in the future because technology evolves so fast that last year's big secret is next year's so-what.

Having said this, if you're revealing a trade secret, the obligation to maintain the secret absolutely must, without exception, last forever. Once the obligation to maintain the secret is gone, so is your trade secret. No court will protect your right in that trade secret after you've consented to it being publicly revealed.

Moreover, by thoughtlessly signing a generic NDA, which mushes everything together, including your trade secret, you just gave away your company's most important asset. Oops.

CONFIDENTIALITY AGREEMENTS

Confidentiality agreements are the most common type of agreement I write as a lawyer. No matter what type of deal, the parties inevitably want one in place. After doing this stuff for twenty-plus years, here are some tips from the deal negotiation trenches.

Let's start with the common misconception that there is a "standard" confidentiality agreement sitting on my hard drive waiting to be printed. (When I started practicing law, people thought that the "standard" form was in my drawer and I filled in the blanks with a typewriter. Times and technology have certainly changed, but the myth of the "standard" form has not.)

In fact, to the contrary, the confidentiality agreement may be the first "little deal" you negotiate on your way to the Promised Land of whatever it is you're negotiating in the big picture.

However, before we discuss the how-to on these agreements, let me say that I think confidentiality agreements are widely overused. Clients ask me to prepare one before they even have a preliminary discussion with the other side.

My recommendation is usually that preliminary discussions proceed without any agreement in place. After all, why would you want to share secrets with people until you have reason to believe that there's a real possibility that both sides are serious about the deal. Until then, the verbal understanding should be that the parties won't share confidential information.

If and when the deal is getting serious, that's the time to impose a confidentiality obligation on the parties. Remember that most confidentiality agreements have reciprocal obligations. Therefore, in trying to tie their hands with your information, you may unintentionally find yourself restrained from pursuing a direction you want to go because you may be accused of breaching a confidentiality agreement.

Degree of Care

If you're going to be the one mostly receiving confidential information, you want to have the lowest standard of care possible with the other side's information. So here, you want language like, "You will use commercially reasonable efforts to protect the information."

A good fallback position is that you will use "the same degree of care" to protect the other side's information as you use to protect your own information of similar sensitivity. Of course, the beauty of this language is that it is so mushy that it's hard to ascertain what it means. It's not exactly an objective standard.

If you're the one concerned about your own information in the other side's hands, you want to use stronger language. You'll want things like a requirement that the other side not disclose the information except to people with a "need-to-know." You might even limit disclosure to certain named people within the company and certainly no consultants or other third parties.

Have Ready-to-Go Documents

I advise my clients to let me prepare two documents for them. One is for when they have sensitive information and they want as much protection as I can get them. The other is for when confidentiality is more of an issue for the other side.

The reason to have the agreements ready to go is that when a deal is at the stage that it's now appropriate to sign a confidentiality agreement, you want to quickly volunteer your agreement before they volunteer theirs.

There is usually an advantage to being the one who provides the document.

I've often said, "He who drafts sets the agenda," which is to say that no matter how much you and I negotiate their form, you'll never do as well as when they're negotiating my form. It's just the way it is in the world of sophisticated business negotiations.

Limiting the Subject Matter

If you're not as concerned with your information as the other side is with theirs, you'll want to be as specific as possible about what exactly the confidential information is. You'll want to avoid catchall language and their ability to designate previously disclosed information as confidential after the fact.

Of course, you should flip the advice if you're providing them important company secrets. You'll still want the specifics, but be sure to get yourself some broader language. People being people, they sometimes say the darndest things.

How Long?

There are two issues under the heading of "How long." One is that you may want to limit the period of disclosure so that you can have an intense period with lots of information exchange, but that's it. Anything disclosed outside this defined period, let's say the next 30 days, isn't covered by the agreement. Of course, if you're mostly providing the secrets, you'll want as long a period as you can get.

The second issue is how long the confidentiality obligation should last. If the information will be public anyway in six months, you don't need a three-year agreement. You get the idea.

Whatever confidentiality deal you strike, just be aware there is no standard agreement or terms. You're free to strike the deal that best balances your risks with the benefits of the confidentiality agreement. Just don't sign whatever it is they put in front of you because it's their "standard form."

DON'T ACCEPT LIMITS ON OTHER PARTY'S LIABILITY

When clients come to me to consider suing because of a tech deal that has gone bad, the single worst lawsuit killer is often the "standard" limitation of liability clause. It never ceases to amaze me how people don't even pay attention to these clauses as they blithely sign-off on a one-sided agreement. It's just one little clause and yet it can cause so much damage.

Here's an example of the type of provision that you'll see in tech agreements:

"The liability of developer to customer for any reason and upon any cause of action related to the performance of the work under this agreement whether in tort or in contract or otherwise shall be limited to the amount paid by the customer to the developer pursuant to this agreement."

Judges Can Read

Now, if you sign off on a clause like that because you figure that your lawyer will find some technicality to overcome it, I'd say don't depend on it. As a generalization, it means what it says; judges can read and will probably enforce it as written.

If you had to sue for damages that exceed what you've paid under the agreement, all isn't necessarily lost, but it's like fighting with both hands tied. While it's clearly one-sided, courts aren't in the business of rewriting deals to make them fairer.

That's your job when you're negotiating your deal.

It's the Norm

When you negotiate your agreement and tell the other side that the limit of liability has to go, you're likely to get a blank look. You know, it's the same look you get from your kids when you remind them that they haven't given you your change.

I know what I say when I represent the seller of tech services. I say things like "Limits of liability are the norm." "Everybody uses them." "We've never done a deal without one." "We'd have to increase the price dramatically because of the additional risk we'd be assuming."

Ironically, all of this is true. So, we're done, right? Wrong. A skilled and experienced negotiator can make all the difference here.

While it is to some extent the norm to see limits of liability in tech deals, it's not necessarily true that they're all as onerous as my example. While getting the other side to remove it completely may be like climbing Everest, making it fairer isn't necessarily so hard if you ask for the right things.

The Negotiation

If they won't eliminate the limit of liability provision, you have to start pecking at it. In my example, the developer's liability is "limited to the amount paid by the customer to the developer pursuant to this agreement."

Let's say we have a $500,000 deal cooking, which calls for five equal payments over 5 months as work progresses. Let's say that after the first month it becomes clear that the work they're doing is causing more harm than good, so you rightly refuse to make your second $100,000 payment. Finally, let's say that they've somehow caused damages worth $200,000.

You might think that you can sue for your $200,000, but you can't because you're limited to the amount you've paid—i.e. a refund. So, as written, no matter what they do and no matter how bad it is, the most you get is the $100,000 you've paid to date. They risked nothing!

My first attempt to chink their armor would be to ask them to limit liability to the total value of the contract to them ($500,000), not the amount paid to date. Failing that, I might ask for some multiple of the amount paid to date.

Another approach is "reciprocity." In fact, I'd say that no single word is more important in moving a one-sided agreement toward the middle than reciprocity. What's good for them is good for you. Don't be embarrassed to ask. They certainly weren't embarrassed to make it one-sided to their advantage.

The idea is that the most that they can ever recover from you is equal to the most you can recover from them. Why should they have a protective limit, but not you? They won't like that, but it's hard to argue against the proposal's inherent fairness.

Yet another approach is to carve out an exception for infringing intellectual property. In the example as written, if they "create" software for you and you get sued for millions for infringing some third party's copyright, you pay millions, but can only recover $500,000 from the ones who really caused the infringement. Again, it's not fair.

The last thing you might try is to exclude any third party's property damage or bodily injury claim from the limit of liability. As with the copyright situation, it seems inherently unfair that you should pay unlimited amounts of money to a third party because of something your developer did, but then your recovery is limited by your contract.

It's almost a waste of time to put effort into negotiating a contract to have it emasculated by a one-sided limitation of liability clause. Don't let that happen to you. While it may be true that these types of clauses are "normal," don't assume that the one in their proposed agreement has dropped from the heavens as the only way it can be.

CONTRACT MANAGEMENT

Most businesses collect contracts at a prodigious rate. It's almost insidious as the sheer numbers grow. If you stop and consider, you probably have contracts like software licenses, office space leases, maintenance agreements, warranties, website hosting agreements, employee leasing, and agreements with independent contractors. Managing these agreements is essential.

Consider this. No matter how good your agreement is, it's useless to you if you don't know what your rights and remedies are under the agreement.

You can't use what you negotiated to your benefit if you don't know what's buried in your agreement.

It only gets worse as the number of agreements you have grows; the people who negotiated them move to different positions in your organization or worse, move on to other companies. With them goes the institutional knowledge of what your deal is.

Of course, the new person in their old position will find that the old person left neatly organized files with all the agreements within the purview of their responsibility. We also know that during the new person's spare time, she will review all the contracts so that she knows everything she needs to know. Finally, we know that neither you nor me believe the first two sentences of this paragraph.

Real Life

In real life, if the new person is lucky, she finds files organized using the old person's idiosyncratic filing system. As for that spare time review of the contracts, we all know that's fantasyland.

All too often, people manage the relationships memorialized by what may be 25, 100, 1000, or even thousands of agreements depending on the size of your organization "fireman" style. When it's a burning issue, they deal with it. You know how that goes.

Let's say you're unhappy with the company that hosts your website. You try to find that agreement. Is there an agreement? Where is it? You ask around. Nobody is quite sure. If you're lucky, you find it. If you're not, you ask the other side for a copy of it. Of course, now they're wondering why you're asking. So maybe, rather than ask them, you ask your lawyer. Oops, you never bothered to send your lawyer a copy of the final signed agreement although he asked for it several times. If I'm describing your life, raise your hand. (Don't worry, your co-workers will think you are stretching.)

Now, let's say you find it. Immediately, you read it. Hey, I bet you can't wait to explain to your boss that had you sent notice LAST WEEK, which would have been 30 days before the agreement's automatic one-year renewal, you could have just terminated and moved on. Since you didn't know that an automatic renewal date had come and gone, you did nothing.

Now, you have to call your tech lawyer and find out if the service you're getting is bad enough to be considered a breach. Of course, even if your lawyer's opinion is good news to you, if the other side believes they didn't breach, it's "Hello courtroom."

Contract Management Software—
Avoiding the Mess

You got to this point because you made the fundamental mistake of not knowing your agreements. It doesn't matter how good an agreement you negotiate is if you don't know what's on the paper and don't take advantage of it.

If you haven't already done so, your company needs to implement a contract management system. Just a small amount of research on the Net will yield a wealth of information about the alternative contract management software solutions available to you.

If you're not familiar with contract management software, it's simply software that automates managing contracts in a user-friendly database.

At the highest level, you have two paths. You could license contract management software like you license Microsoft Word or you could use the services of an Application Service Provider (ASP) who will provide you access to the software over the Net.

Features You Want

A good contract management system is feature rich. While no system has every feature you might like, you need to evaluate which ones are important to you and then look for the system that best fits your needs.

A basic feature is access to the actual document. My preference is that the software image the signed document so that you see the actual signature and any handwritten changes.

Next, you want to be sure that you receive notifications of all time sensitive deadlines. It's a core function for this type of software.

Other features you should look for include secure storage of all related purchase orders, warranties and other documentation relating to a contract. The software should also be a repository of information for vendor profiles, contact information and expense records. Finally, you also want to look at the software's reporting capabilities.

While the information the software gives you is only as good as the quality of what you input, this type of software can be an invaluable tool in managing your business relationships. If you haven't yet outgrown "ad hoc" as your method of managing your legal relationships, make today the day that your business procedures begin to grow up.

JOINT APPLICATION DEVELOPMENT

As a tech lawyer, I've been doing contracts for the custom development of software for years. As the Net took off several years ago, I started to do agreements for the development of websites. In many ways, these types of deals are similar. At the highest level, they both involve programming and can be mucked up quite easily.

When you begin to examine the literature on computer-related development projects, you can't help but detect a pattern. Projects routinely come in late and cost more than expected.

You'll see studies that say things like two-thirds of all projects come in substantially late and that the average large project misses its planned delivery date by 25 to 50 percent.

All too often, companies jump into outsourced development projects in a haphazard way. When they need speedy development, they choose high-risk practices, like signing a contract that hasn't been thoroughly reviewed, which actually reduces the likelihood of on-time completion. When the overriding goal is saving money, they often look to speed as a key to reducing cost. That's a fallacy. Speed usually drives costs up.

If you want your project to be the one that breaks the late and over-budget pattern, you have to have the guts to begin to do things differently. There is a better way. It starts with the five "ps." "Prior planning prevents poor performance."

Consider this, if you're late for an appointment, is it better to take a few minutes to chart your course, or should you leave the house and figure out your route along the way? Common sense says that you should take the time to chart your path, but many development projects seem to follow the latter method.

Speed is often an overriding goal. You have an illusion of speed if you jump right in and have a flurry of development activity happening.

You feel good having skipped niceties like achieving a consensus within your own organization as to what the software or website will do, how it will do it, and other related issues. You're downright heady about having cut lawyers out of the process so that they didn't have the time to nit-pick at silly issues like warranties, performance standards, and a clear statement of work.

The project is moving! Details like performance and maintainability can wait until the next project. As for testing procedures—you'll know if it works.

But wait! There are better approaches.

One methodology to consider is what's called Joint Application Development (JAD). This methodology takes end-users, executives, tech lawyers, and developers off-site, and away from distractions, for meetings where they work out the details of what the developers will create. The focus is on business objectives rather than programming details.

While these meetings do take time, they will generally shorten the entire process because a clear definition of requirements reduces change requests and haggling later.

An important aspect of JAD is that it requires top executives to be intimately involved in the planning process. This helps ensure organizational buy-in and reduces the approval process for the contract that comes from this process.

JAD also shortens the requirements-gathering stage which, with some projects, can seem to go on endlessly. "What do we want the software or website to do" can lead to endless rounds of e-mails, meetings, and political infighting. JAD gets the key players together so they can get it all on the table and quickly resolved.

Yet another way JAD can shorten the development cycle is by eliminating features of questionable value. A typical ad hoc requirements-gathering process often leads to lots of junk creeping into the project to satisfy the needs of various constituencies.

JAD can provide an effective forum for a full and frank discussion. The more you remove items from the project, the faster it can move and the less it will cost.

To make this process work, you need certain key players involved throughout. I emphasize throughout because JAD should be an intensive process, not a "come and go as you please" meeting.

It starts with the executive sponsor who ultimately will bear the go/no-go decision at the end of this process. Others include the end-user representative, developer, others with required specialized knowledge, and the lawyers.

Lawyers who are skilled and experienced with these types of deals can help facilitate accurate and clear communication, and minimize the likelihood of misunderstandings, which can only serve to slow the process.

JAD may seem like it makes work, but it doesn't. It's a time saver that you should try with your next significant project.

COMMON MISCONCEPTIONS
ABOUT TECH LAW

I'll grant you that tech law is a relatively new legal area compared to, let's say, real estate law. I can summarize the difference this way. When a tech lawyer talks about a case that's a golden oldie, he's probably talking about one that's three years old. For a real estate lawyer, the golden oldie is probably 300 years old. Still, that doesn't make it any easier to explain the fundamental misconceptions even bright and sophisticated people have about tech law. Let's dispel some.

The Internet is the Public Domain

This one's my favorite. If you publish something on the Net, legend has it that it's in the public domain. If this were true, it would mean that you have no copyright protection and that anybody could use the stuff you created for any purpose with or without your permission. Uhh—that's wrong, like really wrong, like get you sued wrong.

I suppose that this one comes from the early pre-commercial days of the Net when it was primarily a playground for academics and government. Myth would have it that in those days, the Net was more like a hippie commune from the 60s than the money-centric, e-commerce, big-company dominated thing it is today.

Ironically, publishing material on the Internet even in the early days didn't mean you lost your copyright. Simply put, publishing material on the Internet does not mean and has never meant that you give up any of the protections that copyright law offers.

While the Net may raise some questions that are uniquely online issues, this doesn't mean that the basics change. Sorry, but you can't copy another website and make it your website. This is true even if you can't find a "©" anywhere on the site.

Defamation

Another misconception is that if you say it online, it can't be libelous. This is another one that could cost you in a courtroom if you're not careful.

If you accuse your competition of bad things that aren't true on your website, in a chatroom, in a newsgroup posting (newsgroups are a somewhat less used part of the Internet world and are analogous to an online bulletin boards), or in an e-mail, you can get sued for libel just as quickly as if you had done it in a newspaper. Digital information counts. It's really that simple.

Be warned—you need to be sure that your employees know that they and you can be sued for libel based on what they say online.

Attorney's Fees

When clients come to see me because they want to sue somebody, they inevitably end their angry rant with "and I want the [expletive deleted] to pay my attorney's fee too." Many people think that if they win, they automatically get their fees paid by the loser. That's wrong.

The general rule in the United States is that each side pays their own attorney—win or lose. What you need to know is that you can often change this rule if you want, but bear in mind that this can be a double-edged sword.

In the tech world, the most important exception to this general rule is that if you have a contract that says something like, "In the event of litigation between the parties to enforce the provisions of this Agreement, the prevailing party will be entitled to reimbursement for reasonable attorneys' fees," a court should award attorney's fees to the victor.

I happen to generally like this provision. I think that it helps keep people honest by adding some risk to litigation. Still, there's no wrong answer on this. Many people dislike these provisions and I certainly can't say that they're wrong. It's a matter of taste.

There is one type of situation where I know I don't want an attorney's fee provision. That's where my client is a deep pocket and the other side is Joe Consumer or their company name is "We're Small and Judgment Proof, Inc."

In that situation, an attorney's fee provision in an agreement is a lose-lose for my client. If the other side prevails, my deep pocket client will pay their attorney's fees. If my client wins, he won't be able to collect from Joe Consumer or the little company anyway.

It's Not the Wild West

It's common for people to say that the Net is like the Wild West. It's the ultimate myth. Rather than being lawless, it's increasingly quite regulated.

Let's say that you have a website that hosted in Florida for a company based in France with a target audience throughout Europe. Further, let's imagine that somebody in Hungary makes a request for information from the Florida-hosted site. Then the Net routes the digital data through four states before its transatlantic voyage. It would be fair to say that you have many jurisdictions that could make a claim to power to enforce their law over that website.

The answer to this daunting regulation scenario is to stay informed about the law and get good professional advice. Otherwise, your missteps could be costly.

ENRON AND DATA DESTRUCTION

Enron. Document shredding. File deletion. Arthur Andersen. Not even J.R. Ewing could concoct what these boys did.

It's one of those law school clichés. "Law is common sense as modified by the courts and legislature." Now, let's take this idea and apply the smell test to Arthur Andersen's recent actions. In case you were in Antarctica over the last few weeks (do they have CNN International in Antarctica?), the Big Five accounting firm Arthur Andersen destroyed many documents relating to their audit of oil industry giant Enron. Of course, they did this as Enron was about to collapse.

Now, my nose is perking up. It stinks in here. Of course, we believe that the destruction of these documents was the innocent act of a completely innocent auditor. The stench is getting worse.

Applying the smell test and common sense, you know that you can't audit a multi-zillion dollar company and then destroy the documents underlying your audit just before the bottom drops out. I'm sorry, but that doesn't take three years of law school.

What were they thinking? The only thing that would seem to make sense is that they thought no matter how bad the flak from destroying the documents, it would be worse if anybody saw the documents. J.R. Ewing where are you?

As dumb as the document destruction was, I'm betting that in our digital data world, it will turn out that it failed anyway. My bet is that if there is a proper and thorough investigation, forensic analyses of things like computers at Enron, Arthur Andersen, and the homes of key people, backup tapes, recycle bins, floppy disks, e-mails, and other digital data will yield a treasure trove.

We're no longer at the dawn of the computer age. It should not be a novel concept that hitting the delete button doesn't mean that you have destroyed your document. My guess is not only will it turn out that the Enron and Arthur Andersen people are criminals, but when the digital evidence starts appearing, we'll learn that they were dumb criminals—not even smart enough to effectively destroy the evidence.

Legally Destroying Data

The law does permit you to destroy data, whether digital or paper. If you apply the common sense and smell tests, you realize that the law has to allow this. The alternative is endless warehouses and data storage centers filled with things that are of no use to anyone. Of course, this begs the question—when can you destroy data?

The simple answer is you can destroy data as long as you have no reason to believe that litigation or a government investigation is imminent.

It's that smell test again. If you can smell the litigation coming, your data destruction will develop its own stench.

What Your Company Needs to Do is Develop a Document Retention Policy

With so much data living on computers, the issues relating to data retention has moved from the realm of the general corporate lawyer into the world of the tech lawyer. A good policy has to not only take into account paper documents, but even more importantly, digital data.

Even the commonly used term, Document Retention Policy, is as dated as the term "cc" to mean "carbon copy." In both cases, the terminology has been slow to change, but I would suggest that you should really call your policy a "Data Retention Policy," since the paper version of the data is just one form of your data and in many ways the easiest to destroy.

Enron and Arthur Andersen notwithstanding, there is nothing necessarily nefarious in having a Data Retention Policy. It serves at least three legitimate goals. It saves valuable computer and physical storage space. It reduces the volume of your stored documents, making it easier to find something when you need it. Finally, if there is no legal obligation to keep data, it reduces the likelihood that somebody on a subpoena fishing expedition will dig up something to exploit in future litigation. All three goals are legal and proper.

To keep yourself on the correct side of the law, the first step in creating a policy is to consider any specific laws that may require you to keep certain types of documents for a specific time. If you're in a regulated industry, like banking or health care, you need to consider specific laws aimed at your industry. You also need to consider things like tax laws in case the IRS wants to audit your tax returns.

After reviewing these preliminary considerations, you have to consider all the different types of data you have and all its different forms. A Data Retention Policy is an essential document for every business, but creating it is never easy. There's always an overlay of business needs, accounting needs, and legal issues.

While it's not a fun task that immediately translates to your company's bottom line, you need to attend to putting together an effective and legal Data Retention Policy. When you're done, if it passes the smell test and you follow your policy, you won't find yourself in anybody's crosshairs if a document doesn't exist, provided that you legally and properly destroyed it based upon your long-standing Data Retention Policy.

ANALYZE CONTRACT BEFORE
CALLING LAWYER

If your tech deal goes sour, you may find yourself evaluating whether to sue to recover your damages. You might find it helpful to do a preliminary analysis before calling a lawyer.

When clients call and tell me they want to sue somebody, the first thing I do is ask for a quick synopsis of the facts. Then I want to see the contract and all relevant documents. To evaluate the strength of a case, on one level, you need to see if the facts are such that the other side has breached the contract in a material way. On a second level, you need to see what guidance and limitations the contract has in case of a dispute.

Obviously, the facts in every case will vary. What you're analyzing is whether what happened in fact breached the written agreement. It's great when the contract is a well-written legal document that describes the business deal with a reasonable level of detail. I rarely get to analyze well-written contracts. Two major factors cause this to be true.

The first one is that well-written tech contracts are less likely to be involved in a dispute. This is because most tech litigation isn't about liars, cheats, and thieves. It's about honest people honestly disagreeing over what the deal is. A good contract means the parties took the time to clearly communicate about the terms of their deal and then write it up in an understandable contract.

The second reason that I rarely read quality contracts is that that there are so few of them out there. The quality of the lawyering I see in my tech world continues to shock me, but that's a whole other chapter. In my review, I would like to find language that I can use to support my client's position.

Depending on what type of case I have and whom I represent, I'll look at things like what was the warranty? Is it tied to any objective standard? When should the seller have delivered the services? Did they deliver what they should have delivered? Did the deliverables work as promised? Who owns what intellectual property rights? Who has to indemnify whom and under what circumstances?

Aside from the facts, I look to the contract to see if it has any limitations of liability that may be applicable. Usually, these provisions are one-sided in favor of the seller of technology products or services. It's common to see limitations of liability that severely limit a buyer's ability to recover more than nominal damages against the seller.

Of course, if my client is the seller, these clauses can be great. The best position to be in is to have a limitation of liability clause that says that my client's maximum liability is some small amount, while the other side (typically the buyer of the services) has unlimited liability. It's especially nice to be in this position when negotiating a settlement. The imbalance of power can be quite "persuasive."

Other provisions that I'll search for are clauses that deal with issues like jurisdiction and venue (what court has the power to hear the suit), choice of law (what state or countries' laws will govern the suit), and attorney's fees (does the winner get a reimbursement of attorney's fees). In a perfect world, I'd hope to find that we can sue in a place convenient for my client and that the law that will govern the case isn't the other side's local law.

What's important to note here is that this was all decided when the parties signed the contract. The lesson is that those miscellaneous clauses, which are usually tucked away in the back of contracts, are important. Consider the difference it makes to you if you're able to sue in your backyard using your local law versus having to seek a remedy in a court thousands of miles away. Experience tells me that these types of "standard" clauses are amazingly negotiable and that you should always try.

Another item that's often tucked away somewhere in the back is an alternative dispute resolution clause. Does the contract require mediation or arbitration before or instead of a lawsuit? If it does, these clauses are generally enforceable.

Never lose sight of the fact that lawsuits are nothing less than a form of legalized warfare. Like war, they are costly in terms of resources, stress, and money—and that's if you win. It's usually preferable to reach a compromise settlement rather than spend years involved with courts and litigation. If suing is your best choice, make sure that you know what to expect in the way of time, expense, and risk before you begin.

If the cost-benefit analysis adds up, then fight it like a war: aggressively and with the will and determination to win.

PLANNING FOR THE END
OF YOUR CONTRACTS

There's an old saying among trial lawyers: Write your closing argument first, and then use it as a guide to present your case to the jury. In short, if you know where you're going before you start, you'll eventually end up where you want to be. I think that lawyers who draft high-tech contracts should tattoo that saying across their foreheads.

Too often in their zeal to get the "big deal" signed, many lawyers draft high-tech agreements by thinking only about the beginning of the deal.

They forget about what their clients will need at the end of the deal and, predictably, completely drop the ball when it comes to drafting provisions that will tell the parties what they can (or can't) do when the contract is over. The problem with this is that the end of a high-tech deal is as important to tech companies—if not more important—than the beginning.

Here's a common example. Go get the last technology-based contract that your attorney drafted for your company. (If you don't have one, or you've never needed one before, just follow along with me anyway. I'm sure you'll enjoy the ride.) Remember when that contract was signed? Everyone was so happy about closing the deal. Money was about to change hands, business was looking up—maybe you even had a celebration to mark the beginning of the deal.

But if your tech contract is like the dozens of tech contracts that I see every month, then it suffers from what I call no-end-in-sight. This terrible condition is caused by careless attorneys who only think about the beginning of the deal, and completely forget where they want their clients to be at the end of the deal.

Some of the symptoms of no-end-in-sight are obvious. If, for example, your agreement doesn't describe how or when it's supposed to end, that's an obvious symptom of no-end-in-sight. It was probably caused by an attorney who paid too much attention to the beginning of the agreement, and gave little or no thought to the end.

But It's the Non-obvious Symptoms that You Really Have to Look Out for

These are the most problematic, and usually don't appear until you desperately need to rely on the agreement. Unfortunately, at that point, you're probably up the proverbial creek and there's no paddle in sight.

If you want to know whether your agreement suffers from some of the less-obvious symptoms, apply this simple test: Assume that the other party to your contract will go out of business tomorrow morning. Remember, for the sake of this test, pretend that after tomorrow morning, it's as if the other side dropped off the face of the Earth. Kaput.

(For those non-believers who think this can never happen, take a stroll to your favorite Web search engine and look for articles about the infamous ASP, "Red Gorilla." Once you believe, come on back and keep reading.)

Now ask yourself: Can your company keep functioning without the other party? How much time will it take for your business to find a replacement? How much will it cost? Who owns the intellectual property rights? Who will provide support for the software or hardware? Can you modify or reverse engineer the software as necessary to keep it running, or does the "License" section of your agreement stop you from doing that?

If your response to one or more of these questions is "I'm not sure," then your agreement is probably terminally infected. (I say "terminally" because the odds are low that the other party will let you go back and modify an already-signed agreement for the purpose of adding exit strategies.) Unfortunately, the harsh truth is that once your agreement is infected, all you can do is sit back and hope that the other party stays in business.

My point is that tech agreements are suffering because the attorneys that draft them have too much focus on the here and now, and not the end. While it may be too late to save your current tech contracts, your future contracts don't have to share the same fate. My advice is to think of the end, first. Before you put pen to paper, take a moment to recite the trial lawyers' mantra, and figure out where you want your company to be at the end of the deal—then work backwards from there.

Chapter Four

The Internet: E-Commerce, Legalities, and Getting Paid

EVERYTHING YOU NEED TO KNOW WHEN DOING BUSINESS ONLINE

This chapter will tell you everything you need to know to do business online and use computers in your business. Your first reaction is probably that it's impossible to fit all that in this space. Well, you're right, but humor me while I cram in as much as I can.

To keep it interesting, I'll do this in the form of a quiz so you can test your own knowledge.

Copyrights

The Internet is the public domain and when you publish something on the Net, you lose your copyright. False.

This is just one of those misconceptions that seem to have a life of their own. Intellectual property laws, including copyright and trademark laws, apply as much online as offline. The Net is just not the lawless Wild West, so please get the idea out of your head.

Libel

If you post a libelous statement on a website, you can't be sued for libel. False.

This second item is yet another example of a popular misconception. Call someone a thief on the Internet or a magazine and you have the same result— you'll be sued—unless, of course, the person is a thief. After all, online and offline, truth is an absolute defense to libel.

Contracting Online

If you put a link on your site that says, "Terms and Conditions of Website Use" and it links to a contract that governs use of your site, the contract is enforceable although the web surfer never read it. True.

Well, it is a true or false test, so I have to say that it's more true than not. However, this is still the subject of some controversy. Though I think most courts would agree that it's true, some courts may not agree.

Be cautious on this point. Although I think that you're more likely to have a winner than loser on this point, don't lose sight of the fact that this is a statistical game. To illustrate my point, I state that I may have been perfectly correct when I told you that there was a 10 percent chance of rain; if it rained on your picnic, I was completely wrong. My point is that you should get some good legal advice on your method of online contracting. Afterall, it is a complex area.

Faxed Signatures

You can't enter into a contract with a faxed signature because a fax is not a "writing," but rather is nothing more than a series of beeps and chirps. False.

On this "beeps and chirps" issue, I have to comment that I don't have enough imagination to come up with the idea that a fax isn't a writing because it's—well—created by "beeps and chirps." For this deeply analytical thinking, we needed a judge from Georgia. Without further comment by me, a mere mortal, I will let the judge speak for himself:

"It may also be added that a facsimile transmission does not satisfy the statutory requirement that notice be 'given in writing.' Such a transmission is an audio signal via a telephone line containing information from which a writing may be accurately duplicated, but the transmission of beeps and chirps along a telephone line is not a writing, as that term is customarily used. Indeed, the facsimile transmission may be created, transmitted, received, stored and read without a writing, in the conventional sense, or hard copy in the technical vernacular, having ever been created."

You just have to wonder about someone who thinks "hard copy" is "technical vernacular." I should just stop here because I'm not sure that I have (in the "technical vernacular") the "bandwidth" to analyze the tremendous depth of thought given to us by this learned court, but I won't stop.

On a serious note, I think that this court completely missed the mark with its decision. People commonly use faxes to form contracts and I think that this procedure is generally fine. Still, in an abundance of caution, there is still something nice about receiving the original signature the next day from your favorite overnight delivery company.

Long Distance Courtroom

Your website could give a court in a far away state or country the power to hear a case against your company. True.

This is a troubling area that calls for some caution because the law is unsettled here, and being hauled into a far away court can be extremely expensive to your company and stressful for you.

You're more likely to run into a problem here if your website takes orders from distant places than if your website is really nothing more than an online brochure. Still, you should consult with your tech lawyer about how to deal with the laws of distant places. Some of the recommendations might include having different websites for different countries to help ensure compliance with "local" law, and creating a user agreement that requires web surfers to litigate any disputes in your local courthouse, not theirs.

That's it. Now you know everything you need to know. Maybe not, but this was a good start and I bet you learned something.

CLICKWRAP AGREEMENTS

As you install software, you're usually asked to click an "I Accept" button. If you're like most people, you click it without reading what you're accepting. Another time you're likely to see this "I Accept" button is when you're registering to use a website. Ever read those? Let's assume that you don't read them (I admit it, I rarely read them). Ever wonder if what you didn't read was enforceable against you like a "real" contract?

If you ever read these things, you might be amazed at what they say. Translated into plain English (a fine art untaught during law school), you will typically find statements like, "No matter what we do and no matter how bad it is, we owe you nothing. Further, we do not warrant the information on this site. While we would like you to believe it's accurate, tough luck if it isn't."

Now, you may be thinking that I'm exaggerating. So, here's what CNN .com actually says in its agreement.

"Subscriber expressly agrees that use of CNN interactive is at subscriber's sole risk. Neither CNN . . . nor any . . . third party content providers . . . warrant that CNN interactive will be uninterrupted or error free; nor do they make any warranty as to the results that may be obtained from use of CNN interactive, or as to the accuracy, reliability or content of any information, service, or merchandise provided through CNN interactive." I think I caught the essence in my translation.

Another typical provision says something like, "If you ever sue us, you must sue us in the court farthest from your home."

All right, on that one, I embellished. In real life, it's more like, "If you sue us, you must sue us in our home state, not yours." The result may just be the same depending upon where they're located.

Enforceable?

I led this chapter with the question of whether a click "I Accept" created an enforceable agreement. When I started writing about technology law in 1996, the answer was a big "maybe." Today, it's a relatively solid "yes."

If you wonder why I qualified "yes" with "relatively," it's because if this were a law review article, it would take me several pages of discussion filled with qualifications and citations before I could reach the conclusion. Since I don't want to bore you with the details, and so I don't have to read e-mail from other lawyers pointing out that almost (notice yet another qualifier) nothing is just a "yes" in law, I say "relatively" and we're all happy.

In some ways, the tougher question involves websites that don't require you to click "I Accept," but rather just have a link at the bottom of the website that says something like "Terms and Conditions of Website Use." Here the idea is that your mere use of the site is deemed your assent to the agreement the website has posted. Here, the cases are mixed. Some courts are quick to enforce these too, while others want things like proof that the web surfer really knew the terms of the agreement and at least impliedly consented. That's a tough burden when we're dealing with Joe Websurfer.

Another interesting issue is unusual terms. For example (and I'll make my point by using an absurd example), let's say buried in the fine print of the agreement is a provision requiring you to sell them your car for $100. I think that a court wouldn't find it difficult to conclude that this "unusual" term is not enforceable while the rest of the agreement is binding.

Your Company's Website

If your company has a website, you absolutely must have an agreement governing your website's use posted. I think that it's a simple equation. We live in a litigious world, plus nobody actually negotiates the posted agreement, plus few people read the agreement, plus you will lose few, if any, customers by posting a one-sided agreement—equals—you must post a one-sided agreement.

If you don't, you lose the opportunity to control your own fate. Why let the law govern your website when you can have a contract your lawyer wrote govern it? Envision the ole Scales of Justice. Now imagine the law written by the legislature on one side and a contract written by your tech lawyer on the other. Which one do you want to govern your site? This should be a no-brainer.

Consider that your posted agreement could limit your liability to some nominal amount if somebody sues you. Further, you could require any lawsuit to be filed in your home court. Better yet, your agreement could require arbitration, which is excellent protection from class actions, since arbitration is about one-on-one dispute resolution, not large classes.

My recommendations are simple. You should always have an agreement on your website. You should require a click "I Accept." If you don't want to do that, then make sure that your site has a conspicuous notice stating that use of the site is governed by an agreement and make the link to the agreement as obvious as you can.

MAKE SURE YOUR SLA (SERVICE LEVEL AGREEMENT) IS A-OK

I hope that you like Alphabet Soup. Ready? If you outsource technology functions to an IT (Information Technology) provider like an ISP (Internet Service Provider) or ASP (Application Service Provider), you need an SLA (Service Level Agreement). Was that sentence fun or what?

An SLA details the service levels you can expect from an outsourcer and the consequences for failing to achieve them. Consequences could include things like credits against future fees and the right to end the contract. Some SLAs add a carrot to the stick by including bonuses if the provider exceeds service levels.

SLAs are not really a separate agreement, but should be an addendum to the main agreement with your outsourcer. While the main agreement will deal with things like warranties, price, payment, limitations of liability, indemnification, intellectual property, confidentiality, and other basic terms, it's your SLA that details things like downtime, response time, lost packets, ping times, and other technical minutia, which used to only interest vampires turned techies. Now, as our reliance on technology has increased, these things interest or should interest CEOs, too.

While smaller organizations doing smaller deals may rely on vendor-provided boilerplate SLAs, the fact is that it's best to avoid these forms if you can. As somebody who sometimes sits on the vendor side of the table and sometimes on the customer's side, here's the scoop from the trenches.

If you're a vendor, you should be sure to create a form SLA. It should be tilted in your direction, but not too much because you don't want to encourage the buyer of your services to negotiate the SLA from scratch. It's a fine line.

Sophisticated customers will always negotiate SLAs, but a form still smacks of legitimacy. If nothing else, it sets the agenda.

Once you create your form, a little subtle tinkering can make it even more effective as a negotiating tool. One thing you should do is arrange it in a two-column format in eight-point type. Then when you provide it to the other side to review, you either should fax a hard copy or, if you e-mail it, send it as a PDF file. I suggest the PDF because it's a file format that's less inviting to edits when compared to a Word document, which is begging your customer to edit it. You do all this to create the illusion of a "standard" form, which reeks of "non-negotiable."

If you're the customer, your response to this PDF should be, "Please send it to me in Word format so that I can work with the document." Just that request sends a powerful message to your vendor. They now know that you are not going to be a pushover and that they're going to have to enter into a meaningful negotiation designed to find the middle ground, if they want your business.

Even form agreements are negotiable. Yes—they're always negotiable.

The fact is that a clear SLA benefits the deal, not either party. From the vendor's perspective, it prevents the customer from having unrealistic expectations. For the customer, it helps to define what they expect as a way of insuring that they get it.

Negotiating an SLA will require both sides to bring their team to the table. At a minimum, each team should include the business folks affected by the deal, as well as their respective technical people, and a tech lawyer.

A good SLA does more than list service indicators and measurements, and lay out the ongoing monitoring and response process. It should also clearly define each party's responsibilities, deal with corrective action and escalation, and include consequences for failure to meet the required service level.

For example, an SLA may measure the user experience. It could require that the screen be refreshed in three seconds after the user hits the Enter key. If you're dealing with financial trading though, you might need to require subsecond response.

The point is that your SLA negotiation is the time to discuss and agree upon performance.

As the customer, the SLA negotiation is your chance to define what it is you expect and create penalties for failing to achieve these expectations. If you don't get whatever you need in the SLA, you'll be in a weak position to demand it from your vendor later.

FINE PRINT NEEDS CAREFUL REVIEW

Advertising circa 2003 can be so technically squeaky clean that it crosses the line into a bad joke. As I was reading my recent issue of PC Magazine, I was struck by a Dell ad. It had five neat columns with computer systems for sale. The sixth column was the fine print. Imagine that one-sixth of the ad is fine, and I mean fine-little-itty-bitty print. Let's look at the fine print and translate it into English.

Let's start with a simple statement in the ad. It says "1-Yr Next Business Day On-Site Service." Now, I don't know about you, but to me that means that if my computer breaks within one year, Dell sends a technician to my home or office the next business day to fix it. Right?

Wrong.

Well, thankfully Dell gives us a footnote to clarify this clear language. It says that, "Service will be dispatched, if necessary, following phone-based troubleshooting." Translated, that means that you had better be prepared to get verbal instructions on dismantling your system, running diagnostic software, and spending what could be two hours plus on the phone with a tech support rep before they will finally conclude that you need the "On-Site Service" for which you paid extra.

Later it even adds that, "Availability varies." Wonder what that means.

I suspect it means that if nobody is available to visit you the next day, they can say, "We warned you when we said 'Availability varies.'"

So, the final translation of "1-Yr Next Business Day On-Site Service" is, "If your system breaks within one-year and after you spend hours with us on the phone acting as our remote hands, if you still can't fix it and we think you really tried, if we have a tech available in your area, we'll send him to your site."

Now, what's interesting is that this footnote for this warranty offers no clarification of "on-site." I would think that includes my home. Well, maybe it doesn't.

You see, in another column I see a warranty that includes "1-Yr At-Home Service." If you're wondering how that's different from "on-site" service, we have to look at another footnote. This footnote talks about "At-Home or On-Site service." I suppose that by negative implication, they come to your home only if your particular system comes with "At-Home," not merely "On-Site" because "on-site" doesn't include at-home. That's clear, right? I suppose so. I guess. . . .

Now, I know that so far Dell has been wonderful in using the fine print to muddle the clear words in the large print. So, just in case you think you now understand what you're getting, I hate to tell you that even the fine print leaves you wondering because it says, "Other conditions apply." I'm glad that they clarified that.

In case you want clarification on anything in the ad, you'll be pleased to know that they do give you an 800 number and an information filled website. The ad does everything it can to encourage you to use the website except when it comes to warranty information. For warranty information, the fine print tells you that you should try to write to Dell—using the good ol' fashioned post office. That's interesting since I found detailed warranty information on the website. Somehow, it doesn't look like Dell wants to make it too easy for you to read too much fine print.

I suppose that if you want the best warranty, you should buy their "CompleteCare Service." After all, we all know what "complete" means.

"Complete" can't have a footnote because then it wouldn't be "complete," right? Well, guess again because "CompleteCare" doesn't include theft, or loss, or damage due to fire. I'm going to call that Mr. Webster fellow and suggest he change that dictionary of his because it's wrong.

If you want to see the details of the "CompleteCare Service," you'll be pleased to know that if you type in a 67-character address into your browser, you'll find all the details except, of course, the related warranties. For warranty information, the website doesn't link you to the answer. Rather, it says, "For a complete copy of Guaranties and Limited Warranties, please write Dell USA, L.P., Attn: Warranties, One Dell Way, Round Rock, TX 78682."

Some systems give you six-months of "DellNet by MSN® Internet Access." Hey, it's free. "Free" has got to be as "free" as "complete" is "complete"—right? Now, if you've read this far, you know that "free" isn't quite what it used to be.

First, you have to register "within 30 days of invoice" and accept their Terms of Service. That's reasonable enough, but did you know that "free" means that "You agree to be billed monthly fees after the initial service period." Translation—they want your credit card number before you can register for your free six months.

Have no fear though. You can cancel at any time. Do you think that they may be betting that you won't remember to call and cancel after six months? Moreover, if you do call, I wonder how long you have to sit on hold waiting for the MSN Customer Disservice Representative so that you can cancel.

I suppose that it's good to know that our American tradition of "the fine print" is alive and well.

ONE-SIZE-FITS-ALL APPROACH TO TECH CONTRACTS WILL FAIL

Horribly written contracts for tech deals cross my desk every day. They are lawsuits waiting to happen.

When a lawyer writes a contract, he should be writing a document that tells a story about the deal, albeit with a tilt toward his client. Often, what I' see isn't a tilt, it's illiteracy.

When I started practicing law about 20 years ago, I was exposed to what you might call "sophisticated" corporate deals. The documents I saw were well-written.

Then There's Tech Contracting

Usually, the first draft of the contract comes from the seller of the tech services. These deals show the wisdom of the 20-minute-old dotcom driving the deal. (All that's missing are pimples on the documents.)

Throw in some rhetoric like, "We have to move this deal at 'Net speed,'" and "On the West Coast, they do these deals in a day," and what you have is a nuke looking to explode in a courtroom near you.

It's really a simple formula. Poorly written contracts lead to war.

When people are negotiating a deal, they have a natural tendency to assume that the team putting it together will be the team implementing it. I start from the opposite perspective.

I always assume that none of the players at the negotiating table will be involved after the parties sign the contract. Businesses are sold all the time and people get promoted.

When these things happen, it means that whoever knew what the contract "really" meant is gone. The written document has to stand on its own.

When the person across the table doesn't want to take the time to clarify a clause, he'll often say something like, "Come on, you and I know what it means. Just trust me."

At that point, I like to say, "I assume that you're so good at what you do that you'll be out of here doing bigger and better things in about four minutes. It's not you I don't trust. It's the guy who I don't know who will replace you that I don't trust."

You know you have a well-written contract if somebody who knows nothing about the specifics of your deal could read it and understand the deal. If your contract doesn't meet this standard, you need to get one that does.

Let's Do a Reality Check. Why are Tech Contracts Often So Bad?

For starters, tech contracting is a relatively new legal specialty. Outside of a few places like Silicon Valley and Boston, you just can't find many lawyers with legitimate experience doing these deals.

The potential client asking about the experience might have the audacity to think legitimate experience means having done several of these deals.

Before you think lawyers are completely at fault for bad tech contracting practices, let me assure you that's not true. Many times, the first draft has never crossed a lawyer's desk.

After all, why involve your tech lawyer when you have the contract form that somebody else in your industry used or have the contract your lawyer gave you for a different deal?

As for the answers, we could start with one size doesn't fit all and you're playing with fire. While it's tempting to use the form your competitor used, you really don't know that it's any good. The odds are that it isn't.

If you're on the buying side of a tech deal, you should have your tech lawyer prepare the contract from scratch.

If your tech deal is worth doing, it's worth doing right.

If you're buying tech services, you should demand that the other side agree to high-quality legal documents. If excellent documentation of your deal doesn't seem important to them, you should question at what point high-quality will become important to them.

LEGAL IMPLICATIONS FOR DOMAIN NAMES: DISPUTES AND RESOLUTIONS

Before you register that domain name, you need to consider the legal implications of what you're about to do. If you don't, you could find yourself landing in a courtroom.

The days when the law surrounding domain names was as simple as first come, first served are gone forever. The days when the law was still developing and nobody really knew if you could get away with registering mcdonalds .com if McDonald's hadn't already done so are no more. It was the Wild West.

In 1994, Joshua Quittner, of Wired magazine, was writing a story like this one about domain names and discovered that Ronald had not yet understood the importance of registering mcdonalds.com. Reportedly, he even called Ronald's managers to warn them that anyone could register their name if they didn't.

Ronald didn't respond so Joshua did. He registered mcdonalds.com. Josh even adopted the e-mail address Ronald@mcdonalds.com for himself.

Arising from its stupor, McDonald's was not happy when officials realized the significance of what Josh had done. Maybe with Holiday Spirit in mind,

Josh gave the domain to McDonald's in return for a $3,500 donation to an elementary school.

My all-time favorite domain name story involves Princeton Review and Kaplan, bitter competitors in the test preparation business. They prepare you for tests like the SATs for college admission and the LSATs for law school admission.

I bet you know where this is going. Princeton Review not only registered princetonreview.com and review.com, but also kaplan.com.

In 1994, it simply wasn't clear that registering the trademarked name of your competitor was a no-no. You have to admire Princeton Review's ingenuity. This is about the same time McDonalds hadn't yet figured out that it might want to own mcdonalds.com.

Of course, Kaplan soon discovered that people who typed www.kaplan.com were going to Princeton Review's website. Kaplan was perturbed. When challenged, Princeton Review offered the domain to Kaplan for a case of beer (reportedly domestic or imported). Kaplan refused and went to court instead. The court awarded Kaplan the disputed domain.

When it was all over, Princeton Review's president, John Katzman, is reported to have said that Kaplan has "no sense of humor, no vision and no beer."

That was Then and This is Now

You're looking for nothing but trouble if you don't do your homework before you register a domain. The starting point is the Patent and Trademark Office at www.uspto.gov/web/menu/tm.html.

If you get an "all clear" from this search, you still need to have your tech lawyer run and then interpret a full trademark search done by one of many private companies that provide this service. Trademarks can be a treacherous area and I caution you that you do need a lawyer's assistance with this.

The penalty for choosing a problematic domain name is that you may find yourself accused of being a "cybersquatter." Loosely defined before the recently enacted Anti-cybersquatting Consumer Protection Act, a cybersquatter is somebody who registers a domain name for improper purposes, like extorting money from its rightful owner. Of course, the interesting part is giving some meaning to terms like "improper" and "rightful."

The act takes a stab at these terms by saying that several things are improper. For example, it's improper for you to use another's trademark or personal name with a "bad faith intent" to make a profit. It's also improper for you to register, traffic, or use a domain name that's the same or confus-

ingly similar to a mark that was distinctive or famous at the time you registered the name.

A court will use many factors to determine bad faith intent. One part of
the analysis is for the court to see if you have any trademark or other intellectual property rights in the domain name. Other factors include the extent to
which your legal name is represented by the domain name, your previous use
of the domain name in "bona fide" commerce, your "bona fide noncommer-
cial use or fair use" of the mark, your intent to divert consumers from the
proper online site, and using false or misleading information when registering
or holding the mark.

If a court finds that you're a cybersquatter, it could award the rightful
owner substantial damages. Having said that, even with the act in place, many
times it's still unclear who has what rights to what domain name. As is often
the case, the law can be a bit gray.

From practical experience, I've learned if the law's application to your situation is in any way muddy, it still often comes down to a straight price negotiation. If you already have a questionable domain name, you need to know
what your rights are, what your risks are, and then proceed from there.

DOMAIN NAME POACHING

If you currently own a domain name you cherish, you need to be careful
because it's all too easy to lose it. It could be a mistake or fraud, but either
way, you could have a major problem when you discover that you've lost a
valuable domain name.

First, we had cybersquatting, which started in the Net's early days. Then,
you had people who grabbed company names as domain names before the
company with that name registered it. McDonalds and MTV are examples of
famous companies that had cybersquatter problems early in the Internet Age
over their company names. Today, most cybersquatter issues tend to be over
variations on a company name like mtvmusic.net.

Now, enter the poachers. They grab domain names when a domain name
that a company had previously registered becomes available for any of a multitude of reasons. It could be things like a company letting their registration
expire by mistake, domain name registrar error and sometimes, hard to identify shenanigans.

In yet another example of law always developing after the new technologies it regulates, there's little clear law on the issues that arise from domain
name poaching. For instance, let's say the reason a domain name became
available was registrar error. Should the name go back to the original owner?

Would it matter if the name were trademarked? What should the answer be if it's a generic word like lawyer.com?

King for a Day

Before you answer the questions, take a moment to consider how valuable a domain name can be and then, since the law is unsettled, let's play King and decide what you think the law should be.

What if Amazon.com's registration somehow became available—even for an instant—and some association for the preservation of the Amazon forests took it. In creating this fictitious scenario, let's even assume that the problem arose because somebody in Amazon.com's organization mistakenly forgot to pay the fee to renew the registration. So now, I've set it up so that it's Amazon.com's fault. Should this be a case of you snooze, you lose? Darwinists would probably say "yes."

Now, let's change the facts. Let's talk about your home and assume that you "forgot" to pay your properties. In that case, the legal system has elaborate procedures in place to ensure that you don't accidentally lose your home to the highest bidder on the courthouse steps. Does your domain name deserve similar protection?

Is your "ownership" of a domain name a "property" right similar to home ownership or is it more like a contract right? This distinction is important because if it's a mere contract right, the law generally provides fewer protections than if it's a property right.

In one infamous case involving the domain name "sex.com," the owner of sex.com sued the registrar when it allegedly mistakenly cancelled his registration. The basis of the lawsuit included claims of breach of contract, breach of a fiduciary duty, negligent misrepresentation, and conspiracy to convert property.

The lower court ruled in favor of the registrar. In its ruling, the court said the registrar did not have a contractual commitment to prevent the assignment of the domain name to someone else and that a domain name isn't property. This was one lower court's take on the issue and not necessarily the last word. The issue remains, what should the law be?

Redemption Grace Period

It looks like we're heading toward a new policy that will provide for a 30-day redemption grace period. During the grace period, the domain name cannot be transferred to any third party. The hope is that this solution will resolve the issue since the domain name owner will presumably notice that their website isn't functioning.

With that as the ultimate notice, it will give the domain name owner time to resolve the issue before somebody poaches the name. I think it's hard to come up with a reasoned argument against this 30-day hold. It seems to achieve a proper balancing of everyone's interests.

Still, there are many poaching disputes already out there. Courts are being forced to grapple with the murky legal issues that arise. If there were a trend, it would be that the registrars generally come out smelling like a rose. Maybe it's because they have good courtroom lawyers and well-written one-sided non-negotiable agreements.

Whatever the reason, the registrars have this nasty and I think, well-earned reputation for arrogance and poor customer service. As a group, they typically personify customer-service organizations with phone numbers like 1-800-WeDon'tCare. Maybe a few court judgments with hefty money damage awards for when they give away somebody's domain, due to registrar error, might make them more responsive. A little accountability can go a long way.

ONLINE DISPUTE RESOLUTION

Whenever you have buyers and sellers, you will inevitably have disputes, and the online world is no different. What the online world lacks but needs is an inexpensive, quick, efficient, and impartial method of dispute resolution. What we have now is a patchwork system for dealing with these issues, and I'm not optimistic that major improvements are coming anytime soon.

Today, when you make a purchase online and then have a dispute with your seller, there is no quick and easy answer to resolving the problem. This isn't necessarily a uniquely online problem either. For example, just the fact that most consumer purchases are for relatively small amounts creates a problem. You can't exactly hire a team of lawyers, bring in three arbitrators and serve subpoenas because your Cabbage Patch Doll arrived without its birth certificate.

Distance and Language

While my Cabbage Patch Doll example might be a bit flip (okay—very flip), it does help make the point that even small arguments need a method of dispute resolution that's perceived as fair to all concerned. Moreover, the online world is different from going to your local store for a multitude of reasons.

We must come up with better ways to deal with disputes that arise online or face the consequences of consumer fear of online buying because of concerns about things like bad service, broken promises, and fraud.

The starting point of why online is different is distance. There was a time that the best check on "reasonable behavior" by both buyers and sellers was geography. If you lived in a small town where everybody knew everybody, the desire to maintain one's reputation helped ensure that buyers and sellers were fair with one another.

One interesting attempt to take the "reputation" check on behavior from the offline to the online world is what a website like ebay.com does. There, you can see how other buyers have rated your potential seller. The idea is that lots of negative comments will cause people to shy away. The flip side is that the fear of negative comments will cause sellers to act responsibly.

Still, the Internet and e-commerce do throw away geography. With e-commerce, it's almost (the "almost" is mostly about shipping issues) as easy to buy from China as your city's Chinatown. Often, a buyer doesn't even know where their seller is. Most people don't know where even a famous online seller like Amazon.com is located.

Then, consider the language issues created by the Net and the reduced relevance of distance and geography. Sure, the court systems in large metropolises like Miami, New York, and Los Angeles have their share of language issues, but that's nothing compared to the language issues if the world is the marketplace.

The Credit Card Company as Judge

Often things develop almost by accident and today's best online dispute resolution process from a consumer's perspective is an accident brought to you by your credit card company. I call it "an accident" because nobody really wanted to make Master Card and Visa the world's judge and jury, but in the realm of small purchases, they often fill that role.

It's a role they evolved into taking because of their practical need to resolve disputes between buyers and sellers when the buyer refuses to pay because of a dispute with a seller. I always tell people to use their credit card, and not a check, when buying online because their best remedy in case of a problem is to complain to the credit card company. In many ways, it is a good remedy for consumers because the credit card companies tend to give the benefit of any doubt to consumers.

Still, it's not quite a system and it doesn't help where a credit card wasn't the payment method. What we need is some sort of universal arbitration system, similar to the credit card dispute resolution system.

Need a Better System

For such a system to work, it will need to be perceived by all as independent and impartial. Systems set up by industry trade groups and other apparently biased organizations just won't pass the consumer's smell test.

It's also important that disputes be decided consistently according to a clear body of law. One system that fails this test is the arbitration system in place for domain name disputes. While they do publish the decisions of these arbitrators, and that could theoretically be useful for researching precedent relevant to your case, publication isn't useful because the decisions are inconsistent and unpredictable.

In many ways, a good system comes down to a right to be heard, a right to respond, a fair hearing, and a decision based on clear legal principles. It sounds easy until you consider that e-commerce is international by nature. Trying to create an international and enforceable system of dispute resolution isn't going to be easy.

I go back to my starting point. I'm not optimistic that it will happen anytime soon. Until it does, a consumer's best protection online remains buying with a credit card.

WEBSITE OWNERS

Whether you like it or not, the utopian days of the Internet being like some hippie commune from the 60s are long over. Folks, it's business now. Where there's business, disputes follow, and then come the laws and the lawyers. Here's a checklist of ten things to consider so that your website doesn't become a reason to create a line item in your budget called "Litigation expenses."

Let's start at the beginning—creating your website. If you pay someone to build it for you, you expect to own it. Right? The surprise is that you don't unless you have a written agreement that says you do. It doesn't matter that you paid for it. In fact, nothing matters except that written agreement. Yep—it is a trap for the unwary.

The second concern is that once you create that website, you're exposing your business to the world. That could be great for business. It could also mean that you could find yourself sued or criminally prosecuted in some state you've never visited or some country on the other side of the world.

If you think that this can't happen to you, you should think again. It can and does.

Being exposed to courts around the world asserting jurisdiction over you because of a website is just one of the many risks your e-business faces. It leaves you having to answer questions like, do you need to comply with the differing laws of all 50 states—and what about other countries.

The third item to consider is privacy issues. The U.S. has few laws (I didn't say no laws!) regulating online privacy. You need to be cautious about stepping on your customer's privacy concerns. You should consider posting a privacy policy on your website. When you post it, be sure to comply with whatever it is that you post.

Your fourth checklist item involves framing and linking. "Linking" is when a web surfer clicks on a part of your website and he is taken to another website. "Framing" is when you have a link that changes only part of the browser display. With "framing," you might have part of the display showing your navigational choices and maybe even an ad, and the rest being a web page from somebody else's website.

If you frame or link another website, you should consider getting that website owner's consent. This is a murky legal area and it's not clear that this is always required. Still, when faced with "murky," I prefer the conservative approach, especially if it's not costly.

The fifth item for your checklist is your "webwrap" agreement. That's the slang term for that link on the bottom of a web page that says something like, "Terms and Conditions." You know—it's the link nobody ever clicks because, well, who cares?

A "webwrap" also describes that agreement that popped up when you registered to use a website. It was the one that you didn't bother to read, but nonetheless clicked "I agree."

Your website must have one of these two. If you ever read somebody else's, you'd realize that this is your best way to impose one sided conditions on your users. Everybody else does and so should you. Your Terms and Conditions may save you someday from some legal hot water.

Item number six on the checklist is to consider whether you may be infringing somebody's copyright with the content of your website. Copyright applies online just like it applies to books and newspapers. When in doubt, get the copyright owner's consent. If you've "borrowed" your competitor's content, maybe you should find new content.

Trademark laws are the seventh item for the list. Like copyright law, trademark law also applies online. You cannot generally use somebody else's trademarked logo, slogan, or whatever without their permission.

Now let's flip the last two around and call it item number eight. You should be protecting your own intellectual property online. Your site should include proper copyright and trademark notices. You should also register your copyrights and trademarks with the appropriate government agencies. You can even copyright your website, so do it.

Next item is to consider advertising, consumer protection and product liability laws. In many ways, your website is an advertisement. As such, it's subject to all the same laws that regulate this area. Consumer protection can be a particularly treacherous area because these regulations may vary by city or county.

Last but not least is that you should consider having a backup and archiving procedure for your website. This way if anybody ever makes a claim concerning your website, you'll have some way to know what was on your website at the time of the alleged problem.

This may seem like a long list of things to consider. It really isn't and you shouldn't be intimidated by it. Never let a legal checklist stop you from making money. You just figure out how to make the money, and then make your tech lawyer earn his keep by helping you weave your way through the legal thicket.

GRIPE SITES

Who would you imagine owns the domain "FordSucks.com?" Would it surprise you if I told you that it was Ford Motor Company? Clearly, Ford owns it to control it and prevent somebody else from posting a "gripe" site there. "Sucks" at the end of a trademarked name is just one common way to post a gripe site. What do you do if your company finds itself at the wrong end of a gripe site?

Gripe sites come in many flavors and sizes. "Sucks" is probably the most popular, but you also have "stinks" as a variation. Starbucks is at the wrong end of what may be the most famous gripe site of all, "Starbucked.com."

These gripe sites raise some interesting legal issues. One interesting recent case involved a Mr. Mishkoff, who registered the domain "ShopsAtWillow Bend.com" upon learning of a Mr. Taubman intending to build a mall by that name.

Mr. Mishkoff's website included information about the mall and a map and links to the mall's tenants' individual websites. In addition, this site contained a link to his girlfriend's company's site ("shirtbiz.com") and to his web design company's site. Posted on the site was a prominent disclaimer that told surfers that Mr. Mishkoff's site was unofficial, and there was even a link to Mr. Taubman's official site for the mall, found at the addresses theshopsat willowbend.com, and shopwillowbend.com.

Well, you know where this is going. Mr. Taubman wasn't pleased with somebody other than him having the domain "ShopsAtWillowBend.com," so he sued Mr. Mishkoff.

Now, the ball was in Mr. Mishkoff's hands and he responded by registering taubmansucks.com, shopsatwillowbendsucks.com, theshopsatwillowbend sucks.com, willowbendmallsucks.com and willowbendsucks.com. Clearly, Mr. Mishkoff is not a man who's shy about taking on a battle. You can just feel the blood pressure of the parties going up as the situation unfolds and of course, the "sucks" sites become part of the courtroom fray.

These five web names all linked to the same website. According to the court, the content of the site includes a "running editorial on Mishkoff's battle with Taubman and its lawyers, and exhaustively documents his proceedings in both the district court and this Court, both through visual scans of filed motions, as well as a first person narrative from Mishkoff."

The court ruled in favor of Mr. Mishkoff on the "sucks" sites, finding that they were an expression of free speech.

The court said that "[Al]though economic damage might be an intended effect of Mishkoff's expression, the First Amendment protects critical commentary when there is no confusion as to source, even when it involves the criticism of a business." The court then goes on to say that "[i]n fact, Taubman concedes that Mishkoff is 'free to shout 'Taubman Sucks!' from the rooftops . . . ' Essentially, this is what he has done in his domain name. The rooftops of our past have evolved into the Internet domain names of our present. We find that the domain name is a type of public expression, no different in scope than a billboard or a pulpit, and Mishkoff has a First Amendment right to express his opinion about Taubman, and as long as his speech is not commercially misleading, the [Trademark] Act cannot be summoned to prevent it."

So, what are the lessons to be drawn from this case? First and foremost, I would say it's don't get on the wrong side of Mr. Mishkoff.

After that, I take away that you should register the "sucks" variation of your domain names just as Ford did. While there are other cases that do not look so favorably upon the "sucks" site as this one, I say don't rely of winning in a courtroom when a simple and inexpensive domain name registration will do it.

Generally, I advise my clients not to ignore gripe sites. In fact, you should have a Net savvy person assigned to monitoring their possible existence. As you find them, you need to develop a plan for dealing with them. You don't want to be the one to take away Starbucks's title as the victim of the most famous gripe site.

One thing to do is verify and address any legitimate complaint listed in the gripe site. Once you've address the complaint, you might just affirmatively discuss the issue on your site. If you can't make it right from the other side's perspective, then you might tell your side of the story on your site.

Be cautious about cease and desist letters, and other correspondence that has a threatening tone. You're likely to see these letters scanned and posted on the gripe site with commentary that won't make you smile.

As for a lawsuit, that's a big maybe. I can't generalize. These cases turn out to be very fact specific. So, talk to your tech lawyer and then decide if a courtroom is likely to provide a remedy.

PRIVACY POLICY ONLINE AND OFFLINE

Have you reviewed your website's Privacy Policy lately? I know you didn't post it a few years ago, when you first did your website, and forget about it. Right?

If you did, it's time to redo it from scratch. Much has changed in the privacy arena over the last few years. The Privacy Policy you posted may just be a time bomb waiting to explode. The Federal Trade Commission (FTC) has made it quite clear that it will increasingly scrutinize privacy policies and bring enforcement actions.

For those of us who pay attention to this area, the biggest recent surprise was a December 2001 statement by the Director of the FTC's Consumer Protection Bureau. Before the annual meeting of the Promotional Marketing Association, he said that the FTC's position was that it would consider privacy policies posted on a company's website to represent the company's position on privacy—both for data collected online and offline—unless the Privacy Policy clearly stated that it applied only to online data collection.

In my experience, few privacy policies make this distinction because lawyers assumed that if you posted a Privacy Policy online, it only applied to data collected online. This policy change was like a lightening bolt from the blue.

Bear in mind that online privacy policies started largely as a way to assuage the concerns of technophobic newbies to the Net who were worried about what information they might be unknowingly giving away, to they didn't know who, just by surfing the Net. So, privacy policies started as relatively simple documents. I think the first one I did years ago was only about a page long.

These policies have gradually evolved into much lengthier documents, but still the focus has always been on the technological collection of data. Therefore, you often see lots of discussion about uniquely online concerns like cookies.

Before online privacy policies were in vogue, the offline world had long established rules, or maybe I should say it had been long established in the offline world that there were no rules. The fact was and still is that there's almost no privacy legislation in the United States, and you could and still largely can buy and sell customer information like any other asset. If you sell a business in the offline world, you sell your customer list as a matter of routine course. After all, it's a valuable company asset.

Then came privacy policies, increased concern about digital data collected online, a push for more privacy legislation, consumers offended by how their personal information was treated like a commodity, and that brought us to where we are today. Interestingly, despite the push for increased privacy regulation in the United States, the only truly substantial pieces of recent legislation impact only the health care and financial worlds.

I would suggest that unless your privacy policy clearly distinguishes between online and offline data collection and was written this year, it's time to revisit it with your tech lawyer. In fact, this is an area of the law that's evolving so fast that you should consider reviewing your privacy policy at least annually.

In revisiting it, the first choice you need to make is either to clearly state that it only applies to your online data collection practices or rewrite it as a comprehensive policy to address both your online and offline privacy policies. The way to go about this is more of a business than legal decision, but I would just point out that people are increasingly concerned about their privacy. A comprehensive privacy policy may be what it takes to make some people comfortable with doing business with you.

Although privacy is still largely unregulated in the United States, it doesn't mean that your customers and potential customers aren't concerned and sensitive about the issue. I would just suggest that from a business perspective, you just might want to take the high road as a way to win and keep customers.

Whatever you decide to do with your privacy policy, there is one piece of advice that you must follow. Whatever you say in your policy must be completely accurate. Although the law may not specify what your privacy policy must say, the law is clear that you must abide by whatever it is you do say.

So now you have two reasons to reexamine that dusty policy you posted a long, long time ago. One, you want to make sure that you properly deal with the fact that the policy may be deemed your offline policy too—a result you probably did not intend. Two, you want to be sure that it accurately reflects your privacy practices as they exist today.

This isn't rocket science and it's not hard to get this right. You just need to take the time and make the effort.

STAYING OUT OF TROUBLE ONLINE

The end of the last century brought us Internet access in the workplace. While it's clearly a great tool in the office, it can cause problems too. Here are some tips for keeping out of trouble online.

Let's start with the most basic concept. The Internet isn't some lawless subculture that exists outside of the "real" world. What you and your employees do online counts. Your business should have a written Internet Use Policy in place to help minimize the legal risks that could embroil you in unneeded litigation.

For some reason, even reasonably bright people seem to think that "anything goes" online. They couldn't be more wrong.

One troubling area is copyright. A common misconception is that once somebody posts material on the Internet, it's in the public domain. Wrong!

Copyright law applies on the Internet too. Just because it may be as easy as clicking "File, Save" to copy material doesn't mean that it has been donated to you.

While the Internet may raise some questions that are uniquely online issues, this doesn't mean that the basics change. Sorry, but you can't copy your competitor's website, change the name at the top, and make it your website. It's a copyright infringement just as it would be if you did that with their paper brochure. This is true even if they didn't register the copyright with the Copyright Office and you can't find a "©" anywhere on the site.

Another problem area is e-mail. People say the darndest things in e-mail. Things they'd never say in a paper letter or formal memo. Folks who should know better, like Oliver North and Bill Gates, have been betrayed by their own e-mails.

It just may be that e-mail is too easy to send. In many ways, it's as easy as or easier than making a telephone call, so people treat it like the telephone.

Generally, telephone calls are ephemeral and not recorded. E-mail is always recorded. We call the recording device a hard drive. This should be obvious.

Even worse is that "Forward" button. With a few keystrokes, your e-mail could be everywhere you don't want it to be—and you may have no way of knowing that it's there.

The point is that while private verbal communication can often be safely informal, e-mail can never be. Litigants can subpoena e-mails in litigation just as they can subpoena other written documents.

You should always assume that once you hit the "Send" button, it's gone and out of your control forever. You can never really be sure that you've deleted all traces of it and you should act accordingly.

As a businessperson, you must train your employees to be cautious about what they say in e-mail. It should be treated like formal written correspondence in the sense that what you say can come back to haunt them later in a courtroom or the boss's office. (I felt that it was important to clarify the way I meant "formal" because I wouldn't want to be the one responsible for people using fewer smiley faces in their e-mails.)

Using copyright and e-mail as examples, the higher-level point is that you must train your employees about the proper use of the Net. "Common sense" is something mom, dad, and life experience hopefully taught us. When it comes to the Net, you shouldn't assume that your employees have common sense. It's all too new for common sense to have been learned and developed.

It's easy to forget that just a few years ago, ubiquitous Internet and e-mail access in the office wasn't the norm. As an employer, you generally have no reasonable expectation that the people who work for you are experienced Web surfers. What might seem like common sense to those of us who've been online for awhile may not be obvious to the occasional home AOL user. It's all about training.

You have to train people to accept the idea that if they libel somebody in an e-mail, chat room, or on the Web, they can get you sued for it. Eventually, this will be "common sense," but today it's training.

Another troubling area is online contracting. While it's true that the law can sometimes be unclear about whether a contract you enter into online is a "real" contract, you should train your people to assume that it is. It goes back to the basic concept that "online counts."

If you have a policy that limits who can sign contracts for your company, you need to make it clear that this applies to online contracts too. Having said that, this doesn't mean that your offline contracting policy will perfectly fit the online environment without at least some thoughtful modifications. You should consult with your Tech Lawyer on this for the details.

A final thought has to do with adult websites. It's really quite simple. Your Internet Use Policy should prohibit viewing adult sites at the office. (Sorry if I'm killing your fun.)

It's nothing but trouble. Inevitably, somebody is offended. If it gets ugly enough, you may find somebody accusing you of having a sexually hostile work environment.

It's all about training and having a good Internet Use Policy in place. With this, you minimize the risk that providing Internet access to your employees will haunt you.

ONLINE SHOPPING

As you do your shopping online, you "know" that the Internet is a dangerous place for your credit card. Your common sense tells you that it's always better to call the 800 number rather than send your credit card number over the Net. It turns out that what you "know" and your common sense are absolutely and positively wrong.

Understand that I'm not saying that the Internet is a perfectly safe place for your credit card. It's not. But neither is your waiter's or store clerk's hand.

As your waiter walks away with your card, have you ever considered the possibility that he may be running it through his machine more than once.

The fact is that your credit card is never perfectly safe. This is a relative safety, not absolute safety, issue though. Life is all about relative safety issues. If we were seeking absolute safety, we'd never let our kids out of the house.

The Internet has unfairly developed an unsavory reputation when it comes to credit cards. Yes, there is credit card fraud on the Net, but it's a big "so what?" There's credit card fraud everywhere.

I've never understood why the same people who will call 1-800-Send-Me-Some-Junk, read their credit card number to a minimum-wage order taker working for a company they've never heard of, located they don't know where, won't send their credit card number to a reputable store online. Sometimes the things that we do aren't rational.

It'll be our little secret, but have you ever had a store clerk hand you the carbon copy of your credit card charge, torn it into four perfectly neat little pieces and handed it back to her to discard? There you stand—the human shredding machine. It's absurd when you think about it.

People who won't send their credit card number over the Net wear that fact like a badge of honor. It's as if they're the all-knowing ones, and those of us who transmit that magic number are the fools. It's a misplaced concern, and it does matter in the big picture.

It matters because this phobia about credit cards and the Net hurts the growth of e-commerce because credit cards are the fuel that feeds e-commerce. For all the talk about e-cash, online wallets and smart cards, the fact remains that today's payment over the Net is a story that's all about plain old credit cards.

Here's the real bottom line for those of you who would rather wear a big diamond on your finger in a bad neighborhood than let your credit card number traverse the Net. No matter how much money a thief spends on your credit card—whether the thief is a store clerk who "forgot" to give you your card back or that hacker from your nightmares who snatched your credit card number out of cyberspace—you lose $50 at worst.

In 1975, Congress passed the Fair Credit Billing Act (FCBA). Although it predates when I invented the Internet (I wanted to stake my claim here, too), it provides all the protection you need. It's a law that works.

If you follow the FCBA's procedures, your maximum liability for unauthorized use of your credit card is limited to $50. Moreover, if you're a good customer, most banks routinely waive that $50.

You do have to follow the law's procedures to get its benefits. First, and most importantly, send your creditor a written billing error notice within sixty days of receiving the first bill that contained the error. If you look on the back of any credit card bill, you should see a full summary of the FCBA and its procedures.

Now that I've told you to feel free to use your credit card online, please don't take that like a 16-year-old who's been flipped the car keys by dad and then barrels down the road at 90 miles per hour. There are prudent steps you can take to help minimize the risk of online credit card fraud.

You can start by knowing your merchant. Have you heard of them? Are they reputable? There is no magic answer here, but I would suggest that you should have less concern buying from Sears.com than INeverHeardof You.com.

One thing you should look for before you send your card number over the Net is a secure server. A secure server will encrypt your number so that if a hacker were to intercept it, it would be gibberish. Usually, a website will loudly proclaim that you're in a secure server so that you'll feel comfortable using your credit card.

If you have any doubt, you can look at the address bar on your browser. If it says "https" before the address instead of "http," you can feel pretty good about being in a more secure environment.

So, go forth and use your credit card online this holiday season. I'm not promising a perfectly safe journey. There are dangers online, but look at the bright side of online shopping. Nobody will snatch your purse or pick your pocket.

INTERNET MICROPAYMENTS

In early 1997, I predicted that micropayments would become the dominant revenue model for information-providing dotcoms like CNN.com. Using my crystal ball, which is now in the shop for an overhaul, I wrote, "I believe that micropayment-based websites will have more potential for profit sooner than websites that solely rely on advertising."

Reviewing my predictions four years later, it's clear that I was onto something when I expressed misgivings about advertising as a revenue source. All you have to do is read about all the pure online information services like CNN.com that are cutting back and you see that advertising alone is rarely enough to turn a profit.

Now that I'm done patting myself on the back for nailing the prediction about advertising, I have to say that my optimistic predictions about micropayments missed the target by only about 50 billion light years.

In Internet terms, a "micropayment" is an extremely small electronic payment made while you surf. The idea is that while you may not be willing to pay CNN.com 25 cents for every story you read, you might be willing to pay a half penny, especially if the payment process is invisible to you.

In 1997, I wrote, "One of the biggest problems with the Web today is that most companies cannot figure out how to directly profit from providing information on a website." Fast forward to today, and it's still true.

My previous writing continued by saying, "[T]he sale of goods is not what the Web does best. After all, until Scotty can beam it down, there remain just a couple of minor technical hurdles to pulling a new shirt out of your modem."

"What the Web does best is information. The Web is absolutely positively the best way to transmit unlimited amounts of information. The problem—very few companies have found a truly profitable way to sell information using the Web."

Back then, I thought that micropayments could be the most profitable way to sell information over the Net and I still think so in 2003. The problem with my thought is that nobody's making significant money with micropayments.

There are countless reasons for this. It starts with a complete lack of a standardized and simple system to implement micropayments. Until a micropayment system is built into Netscape and Internet Explorer, micropayments don't stand a chance.

The problems continue with consumers not being familiar or comfortable with the idea of paying for content. Let's face it, we all like to surf the Net and get lots of nifty content for free. This party can't last forever though. Something has to give.

It should be obvious to everyone that advertising alone won't be enough to support even the best information sites. What's "giving" today is a cutback in the quality of what's being offered on the Web.

I'm no longer optimistic that micropayments will become common soon.

Instead, I suspect that we'll see an increase in "subscription-required" systems like The Wall Street Journal. With these systems, you'll have to pay a flat monthly fee to get in. It'll be take it all or leave it all.

They won't work for most websites any more than advertising. The problems with subscription sites are endless.

Let's start with the issue of how many sites can and will the average individual subscribe to? If you pay for The Journal, will you pay CNN too? And where does this leave websites with a narrow focus?

Let's say you want a really good movie site because, well it's Saturday night and you're going out. Will you pay a dollar a month for a good movie site if your local newspaper has online movie information ?

A micropayment system resolves these problems. Want to read Dave Barry online? It'll cost you a penny. Want a movie listing? It's half a cent or maybe a quarter of a penny. You don't have to make any big decisions. You just pay in palatable increments as you go.

Don't want to pay? Then tell your browser to not make any payments.

I still believe that micropayments are the way to go—just not yet. You don't want to be too ahead of your time. I think that several years from now, we'll categorize Web history into three parts.

The first-generation Web had lots of free content based on an advertising model that failed. The second generation will have had subscription-based content and it will have failed too. The mature, third-generation Web will be characterized by information being sold online for micropayments. See you in the future. We'll see how my crystal ball did.

TELECOMMUNICATIONS: COMMERCIAL BUILDINGS AND TELECOMMUNICATIONS SERVICES

Real estate developers, beware. AT&T, BellSouth, DirecTV and other telecommunications providers ("telcos") want access to your offices and homes. Telcos want to put their equipment on your property to offer cable television, telephone, and high-speed Internet services.

Many commercial buildings downtown and condominiums recently received proposals from telcos for this, but beware. The "legalese" in these proposals don't protect your rights.

Don't just sign on the dotted line. A real estate developer should provide for consumer choice while protecting consumer safety and community aesthetics. It will make your properties more valuable. It may even provide you with an extra revenue stream. Otherwise, you'll find yourself caught in a complicated mess where several telcos are fighting over limited space in your rights-of-way, conduits and molding, and on rooftops.

To plan for a multi-provider property, you'll need to consider lots of issues including safety, aesthetics, consumer choice, carrier reliability, and general engineering.

You should also look at your current communications revenue streams. Do you charge your telephone or cable television provider a fee for access to your building? Do your occupants receive discounts on services?

Who installed the wiring in your development? Who owns the wiring in your development? Do you even know? Having the answers to these questions is important if you want to get the most bang for your buck.

Traditionally, local telecommunications services have been provided almost exclusively by a single carrier. There was one telephone company and one cable television company. Now the Federal Communications Commission (FCC) is trying to promote competition in the industry.

Recently, the FCC prohibited telcos from entering into exclusive access contracts for commercial property. An exclusive access contract would prevent a building from having more than one telco offering service to tenants. In other words, if you don't like the service from Telco A, you could go to Telco B. But if Telco A has an exclusive deal with a building, and if you don't like the service, you're outta luck.

Now, the FCC has sought comments as to whether prohibitions on exclusive access contracts in commercial settings should be extended to residential settings, and whether this prohibition should be in addition to or in lieu of a nondiscriminatory access requirement.

The FCC has also sought comments on whether it should prohibit carriers from enforcing exclusive access provisions in existing contracts. In other words, the FCC is considering the possibility of "reopening" contracts that have previously been negotiated and entered into in order to allow a developer to reconsider its previous decision to grant a provider an exclusive deal.

Take a look at what companies are providing which services in your developments. Take a "telco inventory" and assess whether your tenants have choices for high speed Internet access and state of the art communications services.

Once you determine what companies are providing telco services to your property, find their contracts. Often, when you look back in your paperwork, you'll see that at one time or another, you probably signed a two or three page agreement with them.

Next, assess the condition of the facilities they installed. On some properties, you'll see that the wiring is rotted and abandoned. Other providers carefully maintain their wiring. Has a provider installed a dish on your rooftop? Have tenants installed dishes in their units? On their terraces?

If you see that the demand is there, issue a request for proposals to see what providers are willing to offer your property. If you own a building in downtown, chances are that your tenants need high speed Internet access and are willing to pay for reliability and 24/7 access. If you've developed a residential community to be inhabited by snow birds, chances are a bulk bill cable television arrangement may be right for your community.

Talk to your anchor tenants. What are the issues that they'd like your help in avoiding? Have they experienced service outages? Have their networks been hacked? For example, if you have a bank as an anchor tenant, you may need to address issues of network security in your telecom agreements. If you have a law firm as a tenant, you may need to ensure that service outages are addressed in minutes or hours, rather than days.

Have you been approached by a company that wants to put a satellite dish on your rooftop? Did you know just how valuable your rooftop space can be to a telco? Telcos are paying thousands upon thousands of dollars to ensure that they can place their reception and transmission antennas at just the right location to give them optimal service, and if that location is your rooftop, make sure that you enter into a properly drafted rooftop lease for the space. (I bet you never thought of your roof as an additional revenue stream!)

Don't let yourself get locked into a dead-end telecom deal. None of us have a crystal ball that will reveal the state of the art service of the future, so make sure you leave your options open.

REGULATING E-BUSINESS, INCREASING CONFIDENCE

Since long before there was an Internet, the Federal Trade Commission has had broad authority to protect consumers by regulating "unfair or deceptive acts or practices." The FTC now takes the common-sense position that consumer protection laws apply online as well.

Internet law being as new as it is, it wasn't too long ago that this position wasn't clear. I characterize the FTC's position as "common sense," but let's not forget the old cliché that law is "'common sense' as modified by the courts and legislature." It's good to see that the FTC has adopted a common-sense approach to regulating e-commerce.

It's the right position for e-businesses and consumers. Adding a dose of consumer protection to the online world breeds consumer confidence. Consumer confidence means more people will buy online. The last thing reputable e-businesses need is for the Internet to develop an unsavory reputation as a place that's less consumer-friendly than other marketplaces.

Let's put to bed the idea that the Internet is the Wild West. It may have been several years ago, when the answer to the most basic questions about Internet law was often, "Nobody knows. The law is unclear in this area." Today, Internet law represents the most rapidly developing area of the law.

As recently as five years ago, I would have said that the body of law that represents Internet law couldn't fill a pamphlet. Today, it's multiple volumes.

It's now clear that the prohibition against "unfair or deceptive acts or practices" encompasses Internet advertising, marketing, and sales. If you're responsible for an e-business, you need to be familiar with the FTC's rules and comply. If you're a consumer, you need to know what your rights are.

The devil is in the details. That summarizes the basic problem with taking old laws regulating Net advertising, marketing and sales, and applying them online.

How exactly do advertisers handle limitations and disclaimers in a banner ad that loudly proclaims a special offer if the offer is complex and cannot fit into a small banner ad?

The fact is that space constraints in a banner ad make it difficult to effectively make proper disclosure. The FTC recognizes this and therefore takes the position that disclosures may be more effective if they're made on the website to which the banner links.

The rule is that advertisers should place disclosures near, and when possible, on the same screen as the triggering claim. The law strongly discourages advertisers from being tricky.

Advertisers are required to use text or visual cues to encourage consumers to scroll down a Web page when it's necessary to see a disclosure. When using a hyperlink to lead to disclosures, the link needs to be obvious. The link should be labeled appropriately to convey the importance of the information that it's giving the consumer.

Consumers who find a website that makes it difficult to understand the "fine print" have a couple of remedies available. They can complain to the FTC. Just as important, they can show disapproval by taking their business to an honest and reputable e-business.

One of the benefits of the Net's rising popularity is that even mid-level and senior government people use it and are increasingly familiar with the way it really works on a practical level. This has often led to reasonable regulatory schemes.

The FTC's foray into clarifying online advertising rules is pleasantly marked by the increasing sophistication of those involved in the regulatory process. They've done an admirable job of making it easier for tech lawyers like me to give clients solid advice based on reasonable and clearer government regulations. Both e-businesses and consumers benefit.

E-businesses must learn the now clearer rules of the game and comply. It's not the Wild West out there and they will have nobody to blame if the FTC makes them a project.

E-MAIL ETIQUETTE IS IMPORTANT

E-mail has to be the best thing to happen to business efficiency since the telephone hit the office desk. Still, it's relatively new and people misuse it and misunderstand it in more ways than I can count. It's time to clean up your act.

While your e-mail software may require you to enter a password, you should never think of your office e-mail as private. If you're the employee, your boss can probably legally read your e-mail. If you're the boss, your information technology department can probably read your e-mail. (Guess again if you thought that you were at the top of the food chain.)

Once you hit the "Send" button, it's gone and impossible to destroy. You just never know who received a forward and what hard drive it lives on.

If you think that e-mail is ephemeral like a phone call, you're wrong. It's more like a virus that you can't cure. A court's ability to subpoena your e-mail is but one way that you may find your e-mail shared with the world. Ask Oliver North and Bill Gates, who are some of the more prominent victims of their own e-mail.

In some ways, I miss the old days when e-mail was new and the few that used it lived by some etiquette rules. Now, it seems that everybody is using it and their mothers never taught them e-mail manners.

The first rule is that sending e-mail messages in ALL CAPS is yelling. Notice that I didn't say that in a lawyer-like way, such as "ALL CAPS might be perceived, depending upon the totality of the circumstances, as speaking in a raised voice, but it depends."

What I said was that ALL CAPS is yelling, because it is. So, don't do it.

Another one that should get your e-mail privileges revoked for a week is a subject line like this: "IMPORTANT—PLEASE READ."

I don't know about you, but e-mails like this always end up being the least important e-mails I read in a day. That's because they're like a bait and switch for unimportant e-mail. If it were truly important, the subject line would read something like, "Evacuate—Kitchen Fire."

The purpose of the subject line is to briefly summarize the e-mail to help your overworked reader, who is bombarded by e-mail, prioritize the importance of your e-mail. Remember when you were in fourth grade and you learned how to pull the "main idea" out of a story. If you wondered why you learned that, now you know: It was because your teacher knew that e-mail would be invented, and she was teaching you how to complete the subject line.

Three-day suspension should be the penalty for the hanging subject line. That's the one where the writer (I use the term loosely here) fits as much of the first sentence as he can in the subject line and then picks it up in the body of the e-mail. Obviously, this is someone who struggled with the "main idea" thing in fourth grade.

Here's the deal on saying negative things in e-mail. DON'T! (Yes, I yelled.)

First, let's look at it like a lawyer. After all, I paid lots of money for my law degree, and I was hoping to use it a bit in this chapter. Negative e-mail is more likely to find its way into a courtroom. The reason is as simple as this: People don't sue each other over happy things.

If you put it in writing, you're creating a record of something you may have to defend once cooler thinking prevails. The heat of the moment has a funny way of playing out in front of 12 bored jurors three years later.

Next, let's look at it from a human perspective. When you say something negative in an e-mail, your reader gets to feel bad when he receives it and every time he rereads it. Further, the written word has a way of seeming so much weightier than the spoken word.

Few people have the ability to tone down their words enough to get the equivalent impact between the spoken and written word. If you say, "That was a dumb thing to do" with an incredulous tone to a co-worker in a meeting, it's probably the equivalent of writing, "Upon reflection, you may realize that the course you chose may not have been the best."

If you think that they're not quite comparable, you're probably right. The carefully chosen written words probably still stung more than the blurted spoken ones. So, if it's negative, get up from your desk and see the person. Don't send them e-mail.

If you forget the details of this chapter, do yourself a favor and just remember one thought—e-mail is forever.

INSTANT MESSENGER IN THE OFFICE

If you've been following the online tech world, you may already know that one of the fastest growing Internet applications is instant messaging (IM). It may have started with teenagers perfecting the ability to have eight simultaneous "chats" going with eight different friends in eight windows, but it has matured into a business application that brings security and legal concerns with it.

According to Jupiter Media Metrix, Inc., approximately 54 million Americans now use IM, including 13 million who use it at work. I suspect that many employers are unaware that their employees use it at work.

In case you're not familiar with IM (which probably means you don't have any teenagers at home), it's Internet software that lets you have real-time conversations online. You type. I see what you type almost instantly on my screen. I type a response. You might call it a conversation. While e-mail is more like trading letters, IM is more like a phone call.

According to the Gartner Group, by 2005, IM will surpass e-mail as the primary online communications tool. Your company shouldn't continue with a policy of benign neglect when it comes to IM. It's here, it's growing, and it's not going away. IM in the workplace requires some thoughtful policy-making.

One of the many issues with IM is security. Right now, the major free IM services (companies like AOL and Yahoo provide the software) have no mechanism to encrypt messages. This means that intercepting your messages would not be that difficult for people like a determined and skilled hacker or corporate spy.

Another issue is authentication. It's all too easy to spoof somebody's name using IM. The corporate world needs security software that will ensure that you are really talking to whoever it is you think it is. I'm sure that it will come soon.

A third big legal problem is logging and archiving. While it's generally illegal in Florida and many states to record a telephone call without the permission of everybody on the telephone call, it's not illegal to save an IM. This is where the paradigm shift from the ephemeral telephone call to the apparently ephemeral IM session can haunt your company.

People often treat IM like a telephone call. They act like it's not going to be saved and that's a dangerous attitude. You might even be the one saving it if you have the archiving feature of your software turned on.

This can come back to haunt your company in a courtroom because your IMs are as discoverable in a lawsuit as your correspondence and other business records. That means that if you don't want to see your IMs shown to some jury as part of a PowerPoint presentation, you shouldn't be saying it in an IM.

A fourth issue, related to the logging and archiving issue, is the entitlement issue. Once you archive an IM, the question is, who can access it? For example, if it's your company, are you entitled to read your employee's IMs? My guess would be "yes," but the key word was "guess." It's not as if I can point to clear law on the subject. The technology is just too new, and law always develops after a new technology.

So, what's a company to do with IM? I say embrace it because it can be a useful business tool. While there are risks, everything has risk. The key is to mitigate those risks in a thoughtful way.

Adopt a User Policy

"Thoughtful" starts by adopting a user policy for IM. Your policy needs to tell your employees what you deem to be appropriate use of IM in the office.

Related to the user policy is education. Your employees need to understand that what they say in an IM reflects on your business and can have legal consequences. Although there's little law yet, you should assume that you could libel somebody in an IM as easily as in an e-mail or letter. In fact, the rule of thumb should be not to say anything in an IM that you don't want to see later and at the most inopportune time.

Education must also include drumming home the concept that people can and do save IMs. Another point is that your people need to understand the risk viruses and related security risks posed with IM. Some experts believe that most firewalls aren't as effective in stopping viruses that penetrate via IM as those that try to penetrate as an e-mail attachment.

Yet another rule is that IM and confidential information don't mix. The technology just isn't mature enough to risk transmitting secrets.

Your user policy should explicitly deal with personal IMs at the office. The problem arises when "excessive" comes into play. I think that common sense is in order here. Consider what your policy is regarding personal phone calls in the office. I would suggest that your personal use of IM policy be similar.

Instant messaging is yet another new technology to enter the workplace. Like all those before it, it brings with it many issues analogous to the technologies that preceded it, and some new baggage. If you give its use in the office the thoughtful attention it deserves, you may find that you have a new and useful tool on your employee's desktops.

LET'S MAKE SPAM ILLEGAL

Nobody likes spam and yet it keeps filling our mailboxes. People have been talking about banning it since the dawn of the Internet, but it keeps coming. It's time to end this annoyance.

We're talking about spam, the unsolicited commercial e-mail. It's all those "lose weight quick," "get free cable TV," and adult website solicitations you get.

Every year, members of Congress introduce bills. They talk. The press writes. And they approve no new law on spam.

It's incredible to me that Congress doesn't act on this issue. Spam is the toxic waste of e-mail and it continues endlessly.

Interestingly, 18 states have passed laws. From what I can tell, their net effect has been about zero.

These state legislatures have focused their anti-spam laws against spammers who falsify things like the point of origin or routing information of their messages. Many of these states also prohibit the sale or distribution of software designed for the primary purpose of faking the point of origin or routing information of their messages.

These are all good ideas, but a state-by-state approach hasn't worked and isn't going to work. It's going to take a federal effort to help with the problem. Even that's not foolproof because spam can originate from outside the country, too.

My solution is simple. Let's just make spam illegal. We did it with faxes and it's helped although not cured the problem of unsolicited commercial faxes.

Interestingly, the way Congress wrote the junk fax law, you could even interpret it to include e-mail, but it's not being used that way. The law says that, "It shall be unlawful for any person within the United States to use any telephone facsimile machine, computer or other device to send an unsolicited advertisement to a telephone facsimile machine." So far, that wouldn't seem to include e-mail. We generally use the word e-mail to mean something different from a "telephone facsimile machine."

Congress defined "telephone facsimile machine" more broadly than the English language does. Under the law, "The term 'telephone facsimile machine' means equipment which has the capacity (A) to transcribe text or images, or both, from paper into an electronic signal and to transmit that signal over a regular telephone line, or (B) to transcribe text or images (or both) from an electronic signal received over a regular telephone line onto paper."

Hey—e-mails slide right into that definition if you take the time to read it carefully. Still, I feel like I'm the only one pushing to use this old statute this way.

So, we need a new law that's directed right at spam. Let's make sending it illegal. Let's make the penalties huge. Then, the law should encourage class actions and give State Attorney's General and the FTC authority to bring enforcement actions.

I want everyone to have the right to enforce this law. Let's make the spammers miserable. Then, legitimate commercial e-mail that you asked for, like ones from your favorite airline telling you about this week's specials, stand a chance of being noticed and read.

Not all commercial e-mail is spam. The difference between the legitimate and the illegitimate is "unsolicited."

If you want to promote your business online, you should—just do it the right way. People who are interested in your message will be more than happy to opt-in to receiving your e-mails. When they register to use your website or buy something from you online, ask them to check a box if they want to receive offers from you. It's legitimate and good business.

An interesting side issue is, should your web form default to requesting promotional e-mails or not? My reaction is that most people have come to expect it to default to getting the e-mail and aren't offended by that. It's easy enough to check the other box.

Chapter Five

Websites: Development and Upkeep; Laws, Issues, and Solutions

BAD TECH SUPPORT: HOW TO
MANAGE AND ENFORCE IT

My most solid suggestion for dealing with bad telephone support, other than escalating, is hanging up and trying again.

Are you still trying to get that software you received as a gift to work? Still trying to get that new computer to connect to the Internet? You can always call tech support. Good luck and may the force be with you.

I can still remember the days when WordPerfect was the leader in consumer tech support. They had 24 by 7 by 365 tech support on their nickel. Really—you called an 800 number.

Those were the days when tech support people were trained, courteous, and hold times were shorter than the time it took them to release a new version. Today, off-the-shelf software is cheaper than it was back then and one of the things we seem to have lost along the way is good telephone tech support.

Just a few days ago, I had an intermittent problem retrieving my e-mail from my Bellsouth.net account. The error message said that I was providing the wrong password.

Since I could get my e-mail at least some of the time, it wasn't a major problem and I knew that I hadn't forgotten my password. Still, as the problem went well into its second day, I decided to call the Customer Disservice Center.

After a ridiculously long hold (the real reason they invented the speaker phone is so that you can work and hold at the same time), I got my NASA rocket science reject of the day. After she asks me my password, she proceeds to tell me that it's correct. (I knew that, but in her defense tech support people do have to deal with people who think that the CD-ROM tray is a cup holder.)

"OK," I say, "What do we look at next?"

Here comes one of her punch lines. She says, "There is nothing I can do to help you with a password problem" and she tries to end the call.

Fortunately, I had my wits about me and said the magic word, "escalate," before she could hang up. (She really couldn't hang up after the magic word because as they remind you, "We might monitor the call for 'quality control purposes.'" "Quality control?" I can't help but smile as I contemplate that phrase in this context. Who says Bellsouth is a humorless company?)

In case you're not familiar with "escalate" as a magic word in the context of telephone tech support, it means that I'd like to speak to somebody with training. Normally, this is a trump card and you go up the food chain, but she had a twist to this I'd never heard before.

"I can't escalate," she says.

Now, that was a low blow and I wasn't prepared for that one. I suspect that they had set up a task force, given it a half million dollar budget and six months to make recommendations on how to deal with requests to "escalate." After all that work, and a 1,000-page report, the final sentence of the report said, "Tell the customer, 'You can't escalate.'"

I scrambled for words. She knew she had me staggered. As she was about to end the call, I mumbled, "Who can escalate?"

I had her now. As she was going down, she said, "My manager."

"OK then, let me speak to your manager." I had won the round.

On hold I go. After several more minutes, she comes back on to tell me that the problem has already been escalated because they had determined that they had a problem with their e-mail server. (They fixed it during the third day.)

Now that I had a reasonable answer, I hung up, but did pause to wonder whether people like her even care that they are so bad at what they do. I suspect they probably don't. It's a paycheck.

Over the years, I think I've heard just about every annoying thing tech support can say. Here are some of my favorites:

"You're the first person to report that problem." Why do they have to say that? It's so annoying, and I don't believe them anyway.

"We're expecting a maintenance release soon, which we hope will address that issue."

I've usually found that the maintenance release arrives anytime but soon and somehow, it never fixes my bug anyway.

"I can't call you back tomorrow to see if my suggestions fixed your problem. We have no outgoing lines." Translation: Too bad if my recommendations didn't fix your problem. You'll just have to call back again and wait on that endless queue again.

"Sorry, no support by e-mail either." Again, you're relegated to that long phone queue. Thanks for the great support.

My most solid suggestion for dealing with bad telephone support, other than escalating, is hanging up and trying again. Although you'll have to sit through the queue again, you might have the good fortune next time of connecting to a competent person. There are a few around.

WEBSITE HOSTING AGREEMENTS

Once you've built your company's website, you have to deal with hosting it. You could have your in-house IT personnel handle it, but many companies will choose to outsource hosting.

If you do outsource it, you'll need to focus on your agreement with the hosting company to ensure that you're getting what you expect.

You know how this works. The sales people promise you the world. They tell you that you get a pipe as big as the Alaska pipeline with triple redundancy in case of a problem, 24 by 7 by 365 tech support, no downtime, and a commitment to maintain the latest technology.

Then, when you get the agreement (you know, the one that they say is just their "routine" form), it turns out that your huge pipe is more like a 56k modem (which you'll share with other websites they host). The redundancy is "Uhhh, like, you know, we can call the phone company if there's a problem, and we have three different cell phones to make the call with so it's triple redundancy." That round-the-clock tech support turns out to be a pager. And, as for that commitment to maintain the latest technology, well—the contract is silent on that one.

Experience tells me that once you get the contracting phase of your deal, your mission will be to turn their "form'" which, on a good day is tilted toward them, and on a bad day borders on illiteracy, into a fair contract that properly and clearly expresses the deal. Rarely is this as easy a task as you would imagine.

The first item in your contract should be a full and detailed description of the scope of the services that they'll provide to you. Here, you're into nitty gritty stuff like security measures and performance levels. Your agreement should have enough details so that you know that if they do what the contract says they'll do, that your transactions will be safe and that a large number of simultaneous users will be able to get to your site.

You will want provisions explaining the type of access you'll have to your own data and the procedure for updating your site. Will the hosting company handle updates? If yes, you'll want details about format and the scope of their obligations. If you'll be doing the updates yourself, you'll need provisions about the tools you'll need and how you'll get past the security, which is designed to keep people from doing what you want to do—modify your site.

The obvious answer to getting in to modify your site is that you'll have password-protected access. The less obvious issues include things like how many passwords can you have, do they log access, and do they have audit trails to determine who did what to the site and when. These can be important if you ever need to track a vandalism or hacking problem.

A key area of your agreement is performance standards. You want provisions that take the promises that you've relied upon to choose this hosting business and turn them into contractual obligations. Brochures and verbal promises may not cut it if they screw up your website and you lose money because of that.

You need provisions on when your site will be available to Net surfers (usually 24 by 7 by 365), objective criteria against which to measure the performance of their server hardware and software, and detailed information about their telecommunications capabilities to connect your site to the Net.

You'll want to negotiate remedies in case the system fails. Your position should be that you should get more than "I'm sorry" if your B2C (business to consumer) website goes down the weekend before Christmas. Often, you can negotiate for credits toward future hosting fees and other remedies.

Experience tells me that the remedies you can realistically hope to negotiate rarely make you whole. Therefore, your best remedy may be a provision letting you out of the contract early if they don't perform as promised.

These seemingly "routine" agreements are complex and highly specialized. If you don't involve your tech lawyer, you'll have nobody to blame but yourself if things go badly.

WEBSITE AUDITS

Your company's website should enhance your company's image and business. However, it can become a regulatory and legal nightmare for your company if you don't attend to ensuring its legal compliance.

You should have your tech lawyer audit your website. This audit will allow you to identify potential risks and devise a legal compliance strategy that takes into account where you do business and your stomach for risk. Your stomach is important because many of the issues you will address in this audit will lead to gray answers. Only you know if you're comfortable in dark gray, light gray or simply black and white.

I will say this though. If you like black and white, the Net is a tough place to be because Internet law is just too new and the law too undeveloped for there to be much black and white. Speaking personally, I was drawn to the entire area of tech law because it is so gray. I happen to enjoy the intellectual challenge of unraveling a constantly changing and somewhat undeveloped legal area.

The starting point for your audit is to ask what you provide over the Net. Is it goods, services, computer information or what? Do you provide it to consumers or businesses or both? If you're a business to business site, you can often avoid compliance with the sometimes nettlesome rules that protect consumers.

An important component of your audit is to look at the geographic limits of where it is you choose to do business. Do you have a statement saying that you limit your business to customers in certain places only? How do you verify that the customer is where he says he is? The answers to these questions help you determine with whose laws you must comply.

I'm a big advocate of websites providing basic company information. Some of my concern here is legal, but I think it's usually a good business move too. I think it's usually wise to have an "About Us" link that details things like your full company name, location, phone number, and e-mail address. I know that when I'm surfing, I hate not being able to find this basic information. While I understand that you may be hoping that you can deal with all Web business on the Web, you should still provide a telephone number—and it should not take a long wandering journey through your website to find it.

One of the unforeseen penalties for not providing something as simple as an easy to locate phone number is that unhappy customers may find it easier to call their credit card company than you. Then, you end up with a lost customer, a chargeback from the credit card, and a charge back fee. It can be an ugly triple whammy.

If you have an electronic catalog and posted prices, I also like to focus on whether your customer can easily find all the information necessary to make an informed decision. One of the things I consider is does the potential customer have enough information before committing himself to the transaction and giving confidential payment information.

Are your prices posted in a clear and unambiguous way? Is the cost of delivery included in the posted price and, if not, are you clear about shipping costs and time. Are you clear on whether sales tax is included and for what states?

Do you have well written Term and Conditions of Website Use posted? This contract is something almost every site should have. It's your chance to impose a contract that protects your interests should you have a problem with a customer or even a mere surfer who is passing through.

You want to be clear on your express promises, recommendations, qualifying information, warranties, and disclaimers. I like to look at where your notice and disclaimers are located on your site. Are they conspicuous? Are they accessible from every page? Do you require a click "I Accept" on your Terms and Conditions before you allow users to register to use your site?

No audit is complete without detailed consideration of privacy issues. I look at issues like does your site collect personally identifiable information from surfers? Is your site geared to children or does it collect information from children?

Children raise their own unique set of issues because of the Children's Online Privacy Protection Act. The key age for this Act is under 13. Be careful with compliance with the Act when dealing with kids.

In a similar way, financial institutions must ensure compliance with Gramm-Leach-Bliley, and anything that touches health or medical raises Health Insurance Portability and Accountability Act issues.

If you touch Europe in any way, you need to be concerned with the European Union's more stringent (as compared to the United States) privacy rules.

What I've attempted to do here is to give you a flavor of some of the concerns a website audit will address. It's only a "flavor" because the list of things to consider is long and illustrious. This chapter didn't even touch intellectual property issues and that, like so many other things, is extremely important. My suggestion is to deal with an audit now before you have some regulatory body or court breathing down your neck.

INTERNATIONAL BUSINESS
ON THE WEB

If you want to be big, you have to think big. You say that you want to make your online business truly international; that's great. The Net is a wonderful tool to get you there. Just don't forget that once you, your products, or your website leave the United States, you've become a citizen of the world— possibly subject to the law of places your feet have never touched.

Today, one of the practical limits on countries trying to require compliance with their local law is simply their inability to enforce their rules. China can say whatever it wants about American websites that don't meet its standards, but it's not like they can do much about it.

Still, that's not where the discussion ends either. If we like the idea of local regulation, we could implement treaties calling for international enforcement of local decrees.

Maybe if you think gambling is a bad thing, you like the idea of enforcing American law against websites that allow Americans to gamble in violation of American law. It's a slippery slope though because then you have to be open to enforcing other countries' laws.

What To Do

Today, the state of the law regarding other countries enforcing their laws against your website is uncertain. Here are some practical tips to help you minimize your risks:

- When a person is going to buy from you online, instead of asking her to fill in the name of her country, you can have a drop list of countries to which you have decided you will sell. While people can still view your site in countries that aren't on your drop-down list, you will have available to you the argument that you've taken reasonable steps to avoid doing business in their country.
- If you're trying to exclude particular countries, another possibility is to have a pop-up window that says something like, "If you are a citizen of countries X, Y and Z, it is illegal for you to order our products or view the material on this site." This is especially important because a first-time viewer doesn't know what they'll see on your site.
- Yet another approach is to localize your operation. If you want to sell to France, you could start a website called, "YourName.fr." You could then hire a local attorney to ensure that you comply with local laws. This might help you if you have to defend yourself in a foreign country, especially when used in conjunction with the other approaches.

If you're in a heavily regulated industry, like tobacco or alcohol, just remember that you don't stop being regulated when you go online. If you can't take phone orders for wine from another country or state, you should assume that you can't take a Web order. If you sell to a place where possession of your goods is illegal, you might be committing a crime under their law by shipping it there.

Whatever you do, just make sure that you get some good lawyering before you start doing business in other countries. The law in this area is murky, and therefore dangerous.

DISASTER PLANNING

Experts estimate that every year American businesses lose $4 billion to computer downtime. Catastrophes like Hurricane Andrew and 9-11 should have taught us how quickly an average day can go bad. Have you ever thought about how your business would recover if you lost your entire information technology infrastructure to a catastrophe?

Have you ever stopped to consider all the different ways your computer systems could be destroyed or brought down for an extended time? The list is endless and just starts with freak stuff, stupid stuff, and Hollywood couldn't have written the script stuff. It could be sabotage, terrorism, weather, fire, a power company problem, and who knows what else.

The point isn't even how it happened. The point is that all your computers are dead, your company is bleeding out like a trauma victim, your eyes are glazed over with that deer-in-the-headlights look, and you're frozen wondering what do you do now.

Here's the deal. If you're looking at the rubble and that's the first time you considered disaster recovery, let's just say you missed the party. It's conceivable that your business may never recover from what you lost.

While a mom and pop operation may be able to get away with a disaster recovery plan that's based on a tape back-up kept at a geographically remote site, that's not going to cut it for a large or even medium sized business, and certainly not an e-business.

Often, it's best to outsource your IT recovery planning to companies that specialize in providing these services. Presumably, it's not your core competency and it rarely makes sense to hire an employee with that narrow expertise. While your best in-house IT person may be a good choice to manage this outsourcing project, this person probably isn't really an expert in this extremely important area.

Moreover, even if you had a disaster recovery expert in-house, you still need to outsource because in a disaster, you'll need access to somebody else's computers quickly while you recover your own operation.

You need to look closely at disaster recovery services offered by companies like Sungard Recovery Systems (www.recovery.sungard.com) and IBM (www.ibm.com/services/continuity). They'll do things like consult on designing, managing, and executing an end-to-end business continuity plan for your business.

They'll help you set up back-up routines and take other appropriate steps to ensure you don't lose data to the unexpected. They have plans that will give you emergency access to their computer centers so that you can temporarily move your IT operations there while you rebuild your own.

With a properly set up plan, you declare an "emergency," and a series of pre-planned and pre-tested steps go into effect. The goal—get you up and running again within a reasonable amount of time.

Probably the severest test ever on the disaster recovery industry was the catastrophe of 9-11. For example, by the end of the week of September 11, Sungard says that it had 30 clients declare an emergency. From everything I've heard about the World Trade Center disaster, it appears that the major disaster recovery companies earned good grades for their performance. They appear to have delivered basically what they promised when the worst happened.

If you decide to outsource your disaster recovery, you should be aware that these companies do have their form agreements ready for you to sign.

In my experience, they're reasonably well written documents that describe the services they'll provide you.

Still, bear in mind that they've paid some lawyer good money to write a contract that's protective of their interests. It's not that the contract will be grossly unfair, but the fact is that experience tells me that it's tilted in their direction, is negotiable, and that with some negotiation, you can tilt it back to the middle so that it's fairer to you.

While theoretically they could volunteer a completely evenhanded, right down the middle document, the fact is they won't. Maybe it's because they expect sophisticated customers to negotiate the agreement, so they figure they need to tilt it their way so that they have room to negotiate. Maybe it's because they know a certain percentage of less sophisticated customers won't bother to negotiate the deal and, from their perspective, why not have a contract that's more favorable to them.

Whatever the reason, you should expect a negotiation process with your agreement with a disaster recovery company. You'll often find that the description of services in the proposed contract doesn't quite match what the sales rep promised. You may find nasty little surprises about unexpected fees or performance standards that don't meet your needs.

Every deal is a bit different and it's impossible to guess where the problems will lie in your agreement, but I've still never seen a first draft that was perfect and ready to sign as delivered. As important as their services could be in saving your business in a disaster, let's just say that the day after the disaster isn't the day to read the contract and discover something unexpected about what you thought you were getting.

If you don't have an adequate disaster plan in place, taking care of this problem just might make a good New Years Resolution.

Chapter Six

Employees' Rights, Obligations, and Pitfalls in Litigation

EMPLOYEES AND TECHNOLOGY

I write mostly for management. This week, I'm flipping my perspective and writing to everybody, but management. The theme is a simple one. Things you needed to know so that your computer doesn't become your worst enemy.

Privacy and the Office

Let's start with privacy issues at the office. The generalization is that the company owns the computer and everything on it. It doesn't matter that you may control some passwords. The company still owns the data.

If you want to take the analysis one layer deeper, it's true that my generality has some exceptions. Still, for the purpose of discussing how to keep your computer from becoming your worst enemy, you should accept the generalization as fact.

Another rule of thumb is don't use your office e-mail for personal correspondence because your company can read it. Again, don't confuse having a password with having control. Always assume that the company has a master password that gets management into your stuff. Moreover, as an aside, management should assume that the I.T. department can read their stuff. It makes you wonder who's really in control.

It comes down to this, you have no reasonable expectation of privacy on your office computer—period. Don't rely on your company's Computer Use Policy even if it would appear to give you some zone of privacy.

The goal isn't litigating about your right to privacy with some former employer. The goal is the computer not being your worst enemy.

A related point has to do with deleting data. You should always assume the worst case, which is that once you input it into a computer, you can never make it go away. Sure, we could get into an esoteric discussion of swap files, recycle bins, backups and file wiping, but that's not the point. The point is simply assume you can't make inputted data go away. The "why" is a boring technical discussion.

This means if you don't want your boss reading it, don't type it, e-mail it, or scan it. Don't assume that even a wipe is a perfect solution. Have you considered those backup tapes or your swap file? Those backup tapes are a great example of something you can't control and may be the ultimate reason why you can't be sure that what you've deleted is gone.

You Represent the Company

It's really simple here. What you do on the computer is no different from what you do with paper and pen. It really is uncomplicated as the same rules apply.

You send a letter with a statement like, "She's a thief," and if it's not true, that's libel. Your company gets sued (and maybe you too), and your company loses. You send an e-mail or instant message with libel in it and it's like paper, it's actionable, there's a lawsuit, and you lose.

You like your competitor's website and since it's easy to copy and paste from it, you do. After all, it's the Web, which is like the Wild West and if they didn't want it copied, they shouldn't have put it on the Web. Therefore, you're okay. Right? No, wrong.

Forget that Wild West metaphor. It's a myth. Cyberspace doesn't exist outside of the legal system. The very same laws apply to your Internet connection as to you sitting at your office in front of your keyboard. The idea that once something goes out into the Internet it's in this lawless "place" is ludicrous—yet widely believed. Forget what you think you knew.

This next one should be common sense, but I'll say it anyway. You shouldn't use the office computer to entertain yourself at adult websites. Just assume that both your company and the website you're visiting are tracking your activities. You should just presume that your company maintains a complete log of everything you do on the Web and that FriendlyNeighborhood AdultWebsite.com knows that somebody from YourCompanyName.com visited them even if you don't register or buy the "goods."

Online Contracting

When you visit a website and it asks you to click "I Accept" to an agreement, you should assume that the "I Accept" button makes the contract you're "accepting" as valid as your signature. For example, if you're buying from a supplier online, be careful about the online terms and conditions changing the deal you negotiated with your supplier offline.

One way to deal with it would be to have your standard written agreement say something like, "Notwithstanding the online terms and conditions, the terms of this document shall govern all transactions between the parties." Now, you're covered.

What Law Applies

When in doubt about online law, just assume that the same law applies online as offline. While it's true that there are many exceptions to this generalization, it's a better rule of thumb than the Internet is the Wild West and a lawless place.

EMPLOYEE SURFING STRATEGIES

In the last few years, Internet access at the office went from rare to ubiquitous. With it came new problems for corporate managers to manage—such as employees using the corporate network to visit adult websites, download pirated software, and waste corporate bandwidth and time to recreationally surf.

Here are some interesting and sobering statistics from those who study these things. Thirty to 40 percent of Internet use in the workplace isn't related to business. Seventy percent of all Web traffic occurs during work hours. Seventy percent of employees admit to viewing or sending adult-oriented e-mail at work.

Popular Sites

Twenty-five of the most visited sites during work hours include Amazon.com, eBay, RealNetworks, and Travelocity. I suppose that people are mostly bidding on new desks for the office, watching educational streaming media, and buying plane tickets for their next business trip. I believe that. Don't you?

Experts say employees surfing the Web from their office PCs cost corporate America more than $1 billion a year. The costs are mostly attributable to lower productivity levels and bandwidth expenses.

Then, let's not forget e-mail. It may not be the bandwidth hog that the Web can be, but it's time consuming. The fact is that many employees use their corporate e-mail to do things like write to Aunt Tilly and Uncle Bob. Again, it's all about lost productivity.

There are even sites that are designed to entertain your workforce while you're paying them. One good example is www.IShouldBeWorking.com. When you arrive, the site greets you with "Welcome Slackers!" Moreover, to help those employees you love to hate, it has an "Uh-Oh, It's Your Boss" panic button.

The instructions on the panic button tell your slacker that "If you should be working but you're not, you may need to give the impression that you are indeed busy. The panic button, located in the upper left corner of every ISBW page, bridges the gap between work and leisure. Simply hit the button whenever the need arises and you will immediately be redirected to a helpful, business oriented website."

Productivity Issues

While I must say that you need to get a life if you can't see the humor in this, there is still a legitimate productivity issue too. Oh, and yes, there's potential legal liability for your company.

Don't you just love our laws? You hire some guy. You give him Net access. He abuses it. You get sued. You pay money. Isn't it great to be an American?

Now you're probably wondering how we could get to this. One scenario could be the "boys" deciding that Joe's office is the place to hang during lunch while Joe gives everybody a tour of his favorite adult websites. When the women decide that this has created a sexually hostile work environment—well, you get the picture.

It turns out that recreational surfing not only creates productivity issues, but also can create a host of legal problems. You could find that your recreationally surfing employees are putting you at risk of sexual harassment claims, copyright infringement, and being accused of invasions of privacy.

Many companies have turned to software solutions to control and monitor what it is that their employees do on the Internet.

Let's start with the preliminary question. May your private company control and monitor what it is that your employees do on the Internet? The answer is a resounding "yes." Courts have viewed your office computers as just that: "yours." You can control them. You can monitor them.

Company Policy

One preliminary step you should take is to have all your employees sign a Computer Use Policy acknowledging and agreeing to the filtering and monitoring.

Filtering software prevents employees from viewing certain types of sites. One problem with filters is that they're not as effective as they claim to be. Some experts estimate that filtering software fails to block one out of every five sites deemed objectionable.

Of course, the statistic itself begs the question, "What's an objectionable site?" Answer—it's in the eye of the beholder.

Maybe we just have to accept that United States Supreme Court Justice Potter Stewart was onto something when he declined to define the kinds of material he understood to be embraced within the term "hard-core pornography." He summed it all up by saying, "I know it when I see it."

This just may have to also be the standard for "objectionable" material in the office. The problem with the filtering software is that the one judging what your employees can't see is a software company and their judgments may not match yours or your lawyers.

Another approach is to monitor and record what your employees do on their computers. You might log the websites they visit or even record their every keystroke. It's up to you to determine the tone you want to set in your company and the measures that you think fit the corporate culture you want to create.

While we can debate how far you can and should go in filtering and monitoring employee Internet access, it's clear that unlimited access to the Net isn't a good option for your business. At the very least, you should create a written policy about responsible Internet use. If you don't, you're playing with fire.

ELECTRONIC EVIDENCE

If you've ever been involved in any type of litigation, you know that finding evidence to support your position is one of the keys to victory. As a tech lawyer, I sometimes am asked by other lawyers to look at nontech cases and offer advice on electronic evidence. Electronic evidence can make or break a case—often in surprising ways.

Let's start with the basics. "Electronic evidence" is any information of any type that's stored in electronic form and is relevant to a particular litigation. It might be stored on things like a hard drive, floppy disk or DVD.

When you consider what electronic evidence you might be able to dig up (or what electronic evidence the other side might find when they start chomping into your bytes), you should take into account that every time you touch a computer, you may be creating electronic evidence.

The Power of E-mail

Let's consider a single hypothetical e-mail message that you created using Word and then copied and pasted into your e-mail program. How many places could this thing turn up? Before I begin answering this question, I must warn you that after you read the answer, you may not sleep tonight. Let's start with the good news.

The most obvious place is that the text of your e-mail will be on your hard drive in whatever folder you save your correspondence. If you went through multiple revisions and drafts, it's possible that your word processor saved every draft, every revision, and the name of everyone who touched the document. Oh yes, let's not forget that this is all along with the date and time of the revisions.

So, you're thinking that this is no problem. There's no litigation pending or threatened concerning this document, so you'll just delete the file. Your lawyer even told you that it would not be improper to destroy this particular document at this particular time. The problem is that you may have accomplished nothing.

The document may also exist on your network back-up tapes. Even if you think of it, generally you can't delete a single file from a back-up tape. That's really OK because by the time I'm done tracing the life of this e-mail, you're going to realize that the tape back-up is the least of your issues.

Once you copy and paste the text into your e-mail program and send it, your e-mail will also turn up in the "sent" box in your e-mail program. Some "recycle bins" or "trash bins" on some computers will even save every version of a file as it changes. With this feature, you may find countless versions of your "sent" box on your hard drive. Every time you send an e-mail, a new version of your "sent" box is created and another old one goes to the recycle bin.

If you're wondering why I called the stuff above the "good news," that's because here comes the bad news. It was good news because, assuming that your lawyer gave you the green light to destroy the document, you could control everything I've talked about—until now.

What you can't control starts with your Internet service provider. While your e-mail might quickly disappear from your hard drive, your provider may have their own back-up procedures, which may ensnare your e-mail. Then, the same goes for your receiver's Internet service provider.

And let's not forget the person to whom you sent your e-mail. It will be in her inbox, e-mail program trash bin, hard drive trash bin, and her tape back-ups. For the coup de grace, if she forwarded it, your e-mail may be like a rabbit on reproductive overdrive.

Scope of the Task

The good news for a lawyer looking for electronic evidence is that computers create and store massive amounts of information. Better yet, it's often stored in ways that aren't obvious to an average user.

When you consider things like temporary and swap files (a computer creates them automatically and without a user's control), which may be chock full of juicy information, you realize that finding helpful electronic evidence is a bit like fishing for one particular fish in the ocean. The task can be expensive if not daunting.

A single floppy disk holds the equivalent of about 720 pages of text. Move to a CD-ROM and you've upped the ante to about 325,000 pages. Each gigabyte is about 500,000 pages.

If you're the one looking for electronic evidence, you'll need to hire an expert who's familiar with the latest technologies for recovering deleted computer data. It's a well-known truism that deleting a file from your hard drive doesn't really destroy the data. Deleting a file is more like removing reference to the file from the table of contents of a book than tearing it out and shredding it.

If you want to truly destroy a file or erase an entire hard drive (let's say before you sell your computer), the standard advice has been to use a program that overwrites the old data with random data. The fact is that this isn't really good enough if someone wants to get to your data badly enough. With techniques like magnetic force microscopy and scanning tunneling microscopy, it is possible to recover data that's been overwritten many times.

When you consider destroying data, remember that in some situations it's illegal to do so. Check with your lawyer before you act. Once your lawyer blesses your data destruction, if you really need to ensure success, forget about overwriting data with random data—it's not foolproof . . . but your fireplace is.

Chapter Seven

Piracy and Crime: Schemes and Scams

HEFTY PENALTY FOR USING
UNLICENSED SOFTWARE

How many computers do you have in your office running Word? How many licenses do you have for Word? If the answer to the first question is "many" and the answer to the second question is "not as many," or if you simply don't know the answers, you need to immediately clean up your act. If you don't, you risk hefty monetary penalties.

You must remember one basic fact about software. When you "buy" software, you don't typically buy the copyright to the software. What you buy is a license to use the software.

Every license is different and there's no such thing as a typical license. Some licenses require one license per computer. Some allow you to put the software on a server for many people to use. Others let you use your work software at home without having to buy a second license. The variations are endless.

You know that little box that pops up as you're installing your software. You know—the one that includes the license you didn't read before you clicked "I Accept." I have a suggestion for you. Next time, read it before you click "I Accept." You should assume that it's a legally binding agreement and you might consider understanding it.

License Enforcement

The Business Software Alliance (BSA) is one trade group in the business of enforcing its member organizations' licenses. Its members include low pro-file companies like Microsoft, Symantec, and Adobe Systems.

If you don't have the proper number of licenses for the software you use, your problem might just start with a disgruntled former employee calling BSA at 1-888-NoPiracy. I don't know about you, but I don't know of many businesses without disgruntled former employees.

Simply put: using software without having the proper license is an invitation to financial disaster. It might start with a letter requesting an audit of your software licenses. It could also start with an unannounced raid by U.S. Marshals. Either way, you will wish that you had just simply paid for the correct licenses from the beginning.

BSA will not accept after-the-fact compliance as a way to resolve your piracy. They always want sizable monetary penalties and then they insist on you buying the correct number of licenses after you pay the penalty. It's not unusual to hear of settlements in the range of $50,000 to $500,000. With this much at stake, you should take any inquiry by BSA as a reason to call your tech lawyer. You're playing with fire here.

Settlement is a good option when you consider that if the copyright owner sued you, it could immediately stop you from using its software and get money damages of as much as $150,000 for each program copied. Then bad gets worse when you consider criminal prosecution could lead to a fine of up to $250,000, or a jail sentence up to five years, or both.

Scope of the Problem

According to BSA, in 1999 in the U.S., about 25 percent of the software they studied was pirated. Florida had an above average piracy rate of 30.7 percent, which put it eighth in the nation. The lowest rate was in Virginia (16.2 percent), the highest rate was in Utah (33.7 percent) and Washington, D.C., came in at a below average 23.5 percent.

Internationally, the problem is far worse. For example, in Bahrain in 2000, it is estimated that 80 percent of the software used there was pirated. In Russia, it was 88 percent. The winner (or is that loser?) is Vietnam, where it is estimated that in 2000, 97 percent of all software was pirated. Still, I would like to take a moment to applaud Vietnam for its improvement in this area, since in 1994 they were at a perfect 100 percent. Obviously, they take stealing other nations' intellectual property quite seriously.

Preventing a Problem

One of the most important steps in preventing software theft and copyright infringement is to educate your employees. You need to teach your employees about all software piracy and the consequences for involving themselves in such actions. The best place to start with your employees is the Computer Use Policy.

Another good step is using metering software, which allows you to inventory and track usage of your company's software.

If you find that your company is using pirated software, you can't undo what you did, but you can and must immediately buy the proper licenses so that you are in full compliance.

If you have a server, you should get a server software license that will allow a certain number of users to connect to the network on which the application is stored. It comes down to this: Software companies are serious about reducing piracy. Like with the IRS, while it's true that you may never be caught cheating, if you are, you will have a massive problem. I suggest that you just pay for the licenses. Besides everything else, it's just the right thing to do.

INTERNET GAMBLING AND THE LAW

Ads for Internet gambling are everywhere you look. I've seen them on billboards and in magazines, and I hear them on syndicated radio programs all the time. The strange twist to this is that lots of people (mostly working for the government) claim that Internet gambling is illegal.

If Internet gambling is illegal, how come ads for Internet gambling are popping up more than ever?

The answer depends on which court you ask.

Whenever pundits talk about Internet gambling, the first thing they do is quote from a federal law called the Wire Act. In pertinent part, the Wire Act says that you can't use a "wire communication facility" to transmit "a bet or wager or information assisting in the placing of bets or wagers on any sporting event or contest."

Some states have interpreted this to mean that the federal law prohibits Internet gambling. Others disagree.

One of the earliest decisions to address the Wire Act's influence over Internet gambling came in 1999, when the Attorney General of New York sued Golden Chips Casino, an Antiguan company, to stop the company from offering Internet gambling to New Yorkers.

In its defense, Golden Chips argued that New York had no right to stop Netizens who simply wanted to bet a few bucks online over a game of virtual poker or blackjack.

Before the lawsuit, gamblers downloaded gaming software from Golden Chips Casino, which allowed them to play casino games on their home com-

puters. The results were transmitted back to Antigua, where bets were tabu-
lated.

All betting, it was alleged, occurred offshore, and not in New York. Since
none of the bets were actually made in New York, it was snake eyes for New
York, right? Wrong.

The court held that the transmission of virtual bets over the Internet vio-
lated New York law. Notably, even though the lawsuit only charged Golden
Chips with violating state law, the court went out of its way to say that Golden
Chips violated federal laws, including the Wire Act, as well.

Although opponents of Internet gambling hailed the court's ruling as a victory, not everyone agreed with the New York court. Enter Louisiana.

Back in the 1870s, Louisiana's state-funded lottery screeched to a halt
amid allegations that officials running the lottery were being bribed. Even
though lotteries were the most prevalent form of gambling at that time, the
allegations had a domino effect, and within a relatively short time, all states
terminated their lotteries.

In February 2001, a Louisiana federal court handed down its decision in a
case in which credit-card companies, including MasterCard and VISA, were
sued for their alleged participation in Internet gambling. Among other things,
the lawsuit alleged that the companies illegally allowed Internet casino gamblers to use their credit cards at virtual casinos.

However, unlike the decision in New York, the federal court in Louisiana
held that casino gambling was neither a "sporting event" nor a "contest,"
and wasn't prohibited by the Wire Act. In an act which many say legitimized
Internet gambling, the court dismissed the case against the credit-card companies.

Still, don't go placing your bets just yet. With the exception of Nevada,
which this summer passed a law legalizing certain forms of Internet gambling, state statutes don't specifically address Internet gambling. In fact, most
states still maintain that Internet gambling is illegal under their existing anti-
gambling laws.

So, you may ask, if virtual gambling is outlawed in almost every state, how
come Internet gambling ads are everywhere? The answer: Reality. State laws
that ban Internet gambling are like Holland's laws on marijuana use: They
prohibit it, but enforcement is virtually nonexistent.

Several bills have been introduced in Congress to ban virtual gambling,
but all have been defeated. Internet gambling sits in a sort of legal purgatory,
but there are a few factors weighing in its favor. First, since Internet gambling
is a multibillion dollar industry, there are probably more than just a few lob-
byists who want to keep the law ambiguous. Also, it's still politically incor-

rect to try to tame the Internet with legislation. Given this, you can bet your bottom dollar that Internet gambling isn't going away anytime soon.

ECONOMIC ESPIONAGE

When we think of the Wild West, we think of horse theft as a serious crime. Some people now refer to the Internet as the Wild West. In the Information Age, the new serious crime is information theft (like stealing trade secrets).

Until recently, protecting trade secrets meant relying mostly on a patchwork of often inconsistent state laws, which provided a civil remedy, but rarely criminalized their theft. That changed a bit in 1996 when the then-president signed the Economic Espionage Act (EEA) of 1996.

In today's world, information is often the most important asset a business owns. Yet these assets are extremely difficult to preserve in a environment where gigabytes of secret data fit on a small disc, companies often rely on outside consultants, and where even employees come and go as part of a mobile work force.

On another level, we also live in a post-Cold War world where some former military spies now find private employment and engage in economic espionage for foreign governments and companies.

The EEA started as a law designed to deal with foreign economic espionage. In its final incarnation, it grew to cover the theft of trade secrets domestically.

Defining "Trade Secret"

First, a definition is in order. Generally, a "trade secret" is any information that's valuable because it is not generally known to or readily ascertainable by other people who could profit from knowing it. To maintain its trade secret status, state laws generally require that you take reasonable efforts to maintain its secrecy. Once information is disclosed, you can't claim that it's a trade secret. You cannot put the cat back in the bag.

There are some variations on this basic definition depending on the state. Some definitions require that you use your trade secret continuously in your business or risk losing your legal protections. Some states require actual economic value, while some states protect trade secrets with only "potential" value.

In deciding whether information is a trade secret, courts have traditionally looked at many factors. For example, how widely known was the information outside of the business claiming the trade secret status? How many people knew the secret? What security measures were used to maintain secrecy? How valuable was the information to its owner and competitors? How much effort and money were used to develop the secret? How hard would it have been for a competitor to duplicate the information using proper methods?

The EEA requires reasonable measures to keep the information secret, but does protect potential, not just actual, value. For a criminal statute, it's a surprisingly broad and, in several ways, broader than many state laws. It's also clearly well-designed for today's digital world. It specifically includes both "tangible and intangible" information "and whether or how stored, compiled, or memorialized physically [or] electronically. . . ."

It even seems to cover information that's been memorized with the language "whether or how stored," and "intangible." This is a truly broad definition of a trade secret.

The Crime

The EEA includes essentially two crimes. The first crime involves foreign economic espionage. The penalty is up to a $500,000 fine and 15 years in jail. An organization that commits the crime can be fined up to $10 million.

The domestic theft of trade secrets is also treated as a serious crime. Here, the maximum penalty is 10 years in jail and a fine governed by general Federal law. The maximum fine under Federal law is generally $250,000, but in cases of pecuniary gain or loss, it can be set as high as the greater of twice the gain to the criminal or twice the loss to the victim. An organization can be fined up to $5 million and arguably more based on the twice the gain or loss method that can be used against an individual.

Staying Out of Trouble

For your organization, the flip side of losing your trade secrets is the damage that can be done by your employee using trade secrets from a previous employer to help them succeed in your company. You may not even realize that you're having corporate success because you're using stolen information. To avoid criminal and civil liability, you must develop and enforce a Compliance Plan. Its purpose—to prevent the use of stolen trade secrets by your company.

You're at particularly high-risk if you answer "yes" to two of the following three questions: Does your business focus on technology and information? Are you rapidly growing by hiring? Do you have a significant reliance on consultants, outsourcers, or temporary workers?

If you answer "yes" to any one of the following, you are clearly at high-risk: Have you hired middle and upper-level people from your competitors? Do you use consultants and temporary workers to assist with research and development? Do you have foreign subsidiaries, affiliates, and other foreign operations?

A good Compliance Plan needs to be custom-designed for your business. There is no such thing as a "one-size-fits-all" plan. It must take into account things like your industry and competitive environment, the types of intellectual property at risk in your business, government standards for your industry, and your corporate culture.

The plan must clearly establish a standard of conduct. It must let your employees and others who work for you know what you expect of them when it comes to trade secrets in their possession. If there is a particular type of risk in your industry or company, then single it out for special mention and treatment.

Your plan should also tell employees how to report violations of it. It should create a procedure for investigation and state the consequences of violations.

Most importantly, this is not a cosmetic document designed to be pulled out of the drawer if you're prosecuted under the EEA or sued. It's an educational tool that needs to be mentioned frequently at department meetings and in company newsletters.

This type of treatment may even have the effect of protecting your own trade secrets because you've sensitized former employees to the risks inherent in stealing trade secrets. It's a winner for you no matter how you view it.

CYBERSTALKING AND CYBERTERRORISM: ITS TERROR & MINIMIZING ITS RISKS

Imagine that every time you're in a chat room online, somebody with a screen name that you can't attach to anybody you know says nasty and threatening things about you. Then one morning, you check your e-mail and find about 1,000 e-mails from that screen name that say, "You better look behind you. I'm going to kill you."

Stalking involves harassing or threatening behavior that a person does repeatedly. Cyberstalking takes stalking online. The general idea is that cyberstalking involves using the Internet, e-mail, chat rooms, and other types of electronic communications to stalk another person.

Unfortunately, cyberstalking is becoming more prevalent as computers, the

Net, and technology become larger parts of our life. The Los Angeles District Attorney's office estimates that about 20 percent of its stalking cases involve electronic harassment. The New York City Police Department has estimated that almost 40 percent of its computer-related investigations involve cyberstalking.

People who haven't been cyberstalked can be quick to minimize it. "It's just e-mail." "It's just words on a computer screen." "It's no big deal."

They're wrong. It's serious. There are many cases where cyberstalking has foreshadowed even more significant behavior like physical violence.

You should never minimize capturing the unwanted attention of an unbalanced person. If ignored, the cyberstalker may just get bored and move along. Or maybe not.

Almost every state has a law that makes it illegal to stalk another person. About half the states have specific cyberstalking statutes. As for the states with stalking statutes, but no cyberstalking statute, the language of the stalking statute is sometimes broad enough to encompass cyberstalking.

Florida is an example of a state that doesn't have a cyberstalking law, but does have a stalking law that seems to cover cyberstalking.

Florida makes it illegal to "engage in a course of conduct directed at a specific person that causes substantial emotional distress in such person and serves no legitimate purpose." The things that I've described as cyberstalking could easily pass muster under this law.

Still, every state needs to adopt specific cyberstalking statutes. There are still people who might argue that electronic stalking couldn't be real stalking because, well, it's just electronic. The law needs to be crystal clear that this view is wrong. Stalking, whether physical or cyber, should be a serious crime.

There are some significant differences between offline and online stalking, but they probably won't make you feel better.

With offline stalking, the victim and the stalker need to be in the same geographic area. With cyberstalking, the stalker may be your neighbor or could be half a world away. You can't tell.

Distance is good because it's less likely that the stalker will physically attack you, but distance adds a significant layer of legal complication. Imagine trying to get a prosecutor in another country, who doesn't even speak your language, to take an interest in what your e-mail inbox had in store for you today.

With cyberstalking, it's also easier to encourage third parties to get into the act. You could end up with lots of people e-mail bombing you, impersonating you online to post inflammatory messages, or doing whatever to make you miserable.

Yet another significant difference is that the impersonal nature of the Net may lower the barrier to harassment and threats. It's a coward's dream—the ability to send fear anonymously and long distance.

There are steps that you can take to minimize your risk of being cyberstalked. For starters, never share personal information in public spaces online. Don't use your real name as your screen name. Pick a gender and age neutral name. Let's face it. "Hotbabe 18" is more likely to have a problem online than "Webber."

It should go without saying, but I'll say it anyway. Be extremely cautious about meeting an online "friend" in person. If you choose to do it (real friendships have started this way), do it in a public place and bring a friend along.

Although your first instinct may be to trash the e-mails or other evidence of the stalking, you must keep them for the police.

If the situation doesn't stop, contact the police. Don't be embarrassed and don't blame yourself. The sad fact is that many people don't have all their bulbs burning brightly and occasionally you may find their dim light shining on you. Seek the help you need. You may be in danger.

Thwart CyberTerror with Planning

In World War II, car manufacturers built tanks, entrepreneurs with no experience in shipbuilding built ships, clothing manufacturers became uniform manufacturers, and so on. So too will our e-commerce-sputtering, dotcom-tech economy become a vibrant part of the war machine.

Our economy must be healthy to build, rebuild, and sustain what it will take to fight the coming protracted war. Last week, you needed to guard your information technology systems against cybercrime, sabotage, interception of private e-mail, viruses, denial of service attacks, and other threats just because it was good business. Today, you have another reason—we are at war.

Good business should have been enough reason to act, but for the most part America has done a horrendous job of dealing with computer security.

Nobody knows what's coming next from our enemies, but cyber warfare has been a known risk for years. Back in February 1999, I said: "Everyday, more commerce and sensitive information flows over the Internet. This dependence on electronic information makes for an inviting target for a new breed of terrorist that some are calling 'cyberterrorists'"

I don't quote myself so that you can congratulate me about writing about the risk two and a half years ago. I do it so that maybe I can establish some instant credibility with you.

Cyberterrorism and cyberwarfare are real threats. Could you imagine the damage to our economy if our enemies close Wall Street next time, not with planes filled with innocent people, but by hacking into and disrupting Wall Street's computer networks? What if we all had to stop using e-mail because they found a way to bring the Internet to its knees?

It's a mistake to label our enemies as insane because it makes them seem weak. They're fanatics, but quite sane and extremely intelligent. Never underestimate your enemy in war.

The right way to fight a war is to assume that the enemy is smarter, more capable and better prepared than you are. With this as the starting point, you will never make the mistake of complacency. In war, complacency kills people.

My expertise is technology so that's where I can offer advice.

You must immediately develop your disaster plan with terrorism in mind. Do you maintain backups off site and far away? You must ensure that your information technology infrastructure has state-of-the-art security in place. You should consider greater use of encryption for sensitive corporate information.

PRETEXTING BREAKS LAW

Have you noticed an increase in the number of online companies that claim they can find sensitive information on anybody? These companies say they can uncover hidden bank accounts, Social Security numbers, credit card balances—virtually any financial information on anybody.

But how do they do that? The answer: It's often something called "pretexting." And online investigators who use pretexting are breaking the law.

For the most part, your financial information is private. For example, unless I get your permission, I can't call up your credit card company and find out how much you owe on your credit card, or whether you even have a credit card. Even if I had the desire (or time) to find this out, the credit card company would never release this information to me.

On the other hand, there's a lot of information that I (or anyone else) can find out about you, all of which is public information. The county where you were born, for example, can tell me your full name, date of birth, and parents' names. Sometimes you give your personal information to the world without even realizing it. Your personal information that you provide to catalog companies, retailers, and online stores is often up for grabs. However, in an effort to get even more sensitive information on their targets (and, subsequently, demand premium rates for their efforts), cyber-sleuths increasingly include a process called "pretexting" in their investigatory toolbox. Pretexting is the practice of getting another person's confidential information under false pretenses. Of course, cyber-sleuths don't advertise that they use pretexting. Instead, they make lofty claims that they can get highly confidential information on anybody by merely typing the subject's name into their database.

Don't you believe it. Despite the prevalence of supercomputers and broadband access, there is no single database that contains everyone's confidential information. Instead, many cyber-sleuths still get highly confidential information the old fashioned way—through lies, impersonation, and deceit. In a word, pretexting.

The bad news: Pretexting can lead to identity theft. With the information obtained, a malicious person can damage your credit rating, make purchases using your credit cards, even subject you to extortion.

The good news: To fight pretexting, a federal law called the Gramm-Leach-Bliley Act (often referred to as the GLB Act) was enacted. It prohibits a person from obtaining, or attempting to obtain, your financial information by making false, fictitious, or fraudulent statements to your bank or other financial institution. It also prohibits someone from using lost, forged, counterfeit, or stolen documents to get sensitive financial information.

More good news: The FTC actively enforces the GLB Act. For example, this past year, the FTC screened more than 1,000 websites, and identified almost 200 companies that offered to obtain and sell nonpublic, confidential, financial information for fees ranging from $100 to $600. The FTC's website—www.FTC.gov—not only describes the FTC's efforts, but also offers helpful advice on how you can avoid becoming the victim of pretexting.

AND WEB BUGS

How much private information are you willing to give away for a freebie or discount? Do you mind having all your drugstore purchases tracked for a markdown? People complain about the lack of privacy in our digital world and yet they seem all too willing to give away their secrets for a pittance. Maybe it's ignorance about what they're giving away, so let's dispel some of that.

I haven't seen this as much in South Florida as other parts of the country, but many stores have discount programs that require you to give the cashier a small card with a barcode as you checkout. The barcode identifies you, which gives them the ability to record and study your purchasing patterns. In return, you get a small discount on your purchases.

In some ways, it strikes me as a fair deal. You give the store the ability to market to you better because they know what you like and you get a discount.

The problem I have with this is so few consumers really understand what it is they are giving away. After all, it's not like the drugstore or supermarket has a big warning sign that says, "By signing up for this program, you agree to let us collect personal information about you, use it to our advantage, and sell it to whomever we want, whenever we want."

If you think that can't be the deal because there "must be a law," you're sadly mistaken. There is very little in the way of privacy protection in the United States. Most of your protection comes from educating yourself about privacy issues.

Spyware

It shouldn't be surprising that these issues follow you onto the Net. The biggest culprit is what's called "spyware." Despite the name, it's legal.

It often comes in the form of "free" software that performs some useful function. You want the functionality, so you install the freebie. What you're often not told is that you're "paying" for the "freebie" by letting them spy on your Internet activities.

Defining "spyware" isn't easy. The best definition I've found comes from Steve Gibson, a well-known software entrepreneur. He says, "Silent background use of an Internet 'backchannel' connection MUST BE PRECEDED by a complete and truthful disclosure of proposed backchannel usage, followed by the receipt of explicit, informed, consent for such use. ANY SOFTWARE communicating across the Internet absent these elements is guilty of information theft and is properly and rightfully termed: Spyware."

He goes on to say that, "The number one reason for declaring software to be 'spyware' is that it sneaks into the user's system and communicates secretly. This is never going to be okay . . . .Since the goal is to inform the user, burying this information beneath a mountain of legal mumbo-jumbo, then claiming to have 'informed the user', misses the mark."

Like the barcoded card at the drugstore, spyware isn't all bad. You make a tradeoff between your information and something else of value you're getting. Of course, this assumes that you understand the tradeoff after a full disclosure. As Steve Gibson said, the issue is that spyware "sneaks" onto your system.

Still, "sneaks" is in the eye of the beholder. One product that's received a bunch of attention is the Gatorsm eWallet (www.gator.com). It's software that makes surfing easier because it remembers things like website passwords for you.

The home page tells you that it, "Fills in FORMS with no typing." "Remembers PASSWORDS automatically." It sounds great. I know that it's a pain to fill in those long forms on the Net. This is the answer to not having to type your address repeatedly.

Gator discloses the tradeoff in innocuous language. "The Gator eWallet comes bundled with OfferCompanion separate software—your direct link to some of the Web's most valuable offers." Hummmm.

So, let's jump in what Steve Gibson calls the "legal mumbo-jumbo" to see what the tradeoff is.

In it's privacy policy, "While we don't know the identity of [our] users, [our software] and [we] anonymously collect and use the following kinds of information: Some of the Web pages viewed; The amount of time spent at some Web sites; Response to the ads displayed; Standard web log information (excluding IP Addresses) and system settings; What software is on the personal computer; First name, country, and five digit ZIP code; Non-personally identifiable information on Web pages and forms; GAIN-Supported Software usage characteristics and preferences."

I don't know about you, but the legal mumbo-jumbo seems to say a bit more than the innocuous statement about "your direct link to some of the Web's most valuable offers."

My advice is that before you install any "free" program, you should do some research to learn whether it includes spyware. What's distressing is that while it's easy to give the advice, you may find that its practical application is difficult because these companies labor to cloak their spying.

I occasionally run Lavasoft's Ad-Aware. It's a freebie that detects spyware. You can get it at any major software download site like cnet.com. You may be shocked when you learn more about how your computer is spying on you.

Web Bugs

If I asked you if the website you're viewing has a "Web bug," you might think that I was asking if it had a glitch or problem. Actually, in this context, when I use the word "bug," you should think of a little surveillance device. Did you know websites and even e-mails can be bugged? Big Browser may be watching.

"Web bugs" are an information-gathering tool. They're not new, but they have been getting more attention lately. They upset privacy advocates because they're invisible and people can put them anywhere that they can place pictures or images on the Web. This means that people can bug Web pages, banner ads, e-mails, and newsgroups.

Welcome to the world of spyware. Can you imagine that you actually thought you could surf anonymously? Think again. You can't even necessarily read your e-mail without sending a message back to the sender saying, "I opened your e-mail."

This must be against the law. Right? As Johnny Carson might have said, "Guess again keyboard breath." (If you're not old enough to understand the Johnny Carson comment, I suppose that your parents would be proud to know that you're reading the Business Section.) It turns out that it's really not clear that Web bugs are illegal.

While government agency investigations and class-action suits have put Web bugs under intense legal scrutiny, I can't point to anything that says that Web bugs are clearly illegal. I can tell you that the Michigan Attorney General has shown interest. The "E-Commerce Law Report" quoted him as saying that Web bugs are "similar to Big Brother. . . . People have no idea their thoughts and practices on the Internet are being tracked or policed. We're going after this secret, third party surveillance."

Dangers from Web Bugs

Web bugs are a great asset to spammers because they let them know if your e-mail address is valid. As soon as you open the spam, the spammer gets a message back that says "valid address."

When marketers use cookies (another technology that upsets privacy advocates) and Web bugs, they obtain the Web addresses of pages you've visited. If that's not bad enough, it gets worse because the address sometimes includes your search terms or personally identifiable information.

It's even possible that using Web bugs and cookies together, "they" can track you by your e-mail address as you surf the Net. In other words, the website knows it's you although you didn't try to tell them it's you who is surfing their site.

Are you feeling paranoid yet? Maybe you should.

It's an area that's clearly ripe for Federal legislation. It strikes me as outrageous that my surfing and e-mail activities can be monitored and I don't know it. It's so over the line that I can't imagine any legitimate debate.

Having said that, I'm not suggesting that Web bugs be banned completely. I'm just suggesting that they be strictly regulated with meaty penalties for violating the law. They do have legitimate commercial uses and you may not object to a particular use if you knew it was happening. It's the fact that it's done surreptitiously that's so outrageous.

The Privacy Foundation (privacyfoundation.org) has suggested a multi-pronged approach for Web bugs. While it may not provide the ultimate answer, I would suggest that it's a good starting point for the discussion about legislation.

They start by suggesting that invisible Web bugs not be permitted. Rather, Web bugs should employ a visible, easily spotted icon on the page.

They next recommend that the icon identify the name of the company that placed the Web bug on the page. In addition, the icon should be labeled to say it is a monitoring device.

When a user clicks on the icon, they suggest that she should receive a disclosure that includes things like what data the Web bug is disclosing, how the data is used after it's collected, what companies receive the data, what other data the Web bug is combined with, and if a cookie is associated with the Web bug.

Also important is that users should be able to "opt-out" from any data collection done by Web bugs.

Finally, nobody should use the Web to collect information from Web pages of a sensitive nature. Examples may include pages intended for children or about medical, financial, job, or sexual matters.

Using Web Bugs Properly

Today, the law in this area is uncertain. The fact is that Web bugs are out there, businesses use them (including some of my clients), and they do have some legitimate purposes.

If you want to stay on the correct side of this legally uncertain area and on the good side of those who surf your site, I would suggest that you adopt a policy of voluntary compliance with the Privacy Foundation's multi-pronged approach. With people's increased sensitivity to privacy issues, I don't think that you can go wrong by erring on the "good guy" side on privacy issues.

METADATA TRAPS FOR THE UNWARY

Metadata

When you e-mail a Microsoft Word file to somebody, she may be able to see information you consider private like text you've deleted, older versions of your document, the names of everybody who has worked on the document, and other goodies. It's called "metadata." Do I have your attention yet?

To put it simply, "metadata" is data about data. It's the who, what, where, why, and how about a document. It's also a trap for the unwary.

While this chapter will focus on Word, it's only because almost everybody uses it. Other programs have metadata issues that you need to consider too.

If you're not aware of metadata and blithely e-mail documents, you may be inadvertently giving away more information than you intend. If you're a lawyer, you may be giving away privileged information and creating an argument that you've waived some aspect of attorney-client privilege. If you're a businessperson, you may give away trade secrets. If you're involved in a negotiation, you may inadvertently reveal your negotiating strategy. However you look at it, metadata can be a disaster waiting to find you.

What Can You Give Away?

I happen to use "Word 2000," so my specifics apply to that version only and some of the details like how to access the metadata may vary depending upon the version you use. Still, the generalizations about the examples I mention do apply.

In Word, when you create or save a document, it saves summary information about the document. You can access it by clicking on "File" and then "Properties." You may find information there that you don't intend to give away.

Another interesting feature is "Track Changes." I use it all the time so that all sides of a deal can see the changes made in a document, when they were made, and by whom. The feature can have a dark side if you're not aware that it's turned "on."

This can happen if somebody clicks on "Tools," "Track Changes," "Highlight Changes," and then unchecks the box "Highlight Changes on Screen." Now, the document is tracking changes and you don't know it.

With this scenario, what you thought was a private process of edits within your organization or between attorney and client are there for your recipient to see. Imagine the possible consequences if your recipient could view the wording evolution from "You are a disreputable thief with no morals," to the carefully crafted "Some people have raised issues about the ethics with which you conduct your business and we are somewhat concerned."

Another feature you need to be aware of is the "Fast save" feature. Its bright side is that it speeds up "saves" by only saving the changes and not the entire document. Its dark side is that it saves text you delete from a document and you don't know it.

You can turn the feature off if you click on "Tools," "Options," "Save" tab, and then uncheck the "Allow fast saves" box. In recent versions of Word, the default setting is that the "Fast save" feature is turned off. Still, somebody could turn it on and as easy as that, he may have access to the evolution of your document.

Another possible information leak can occur because Word saves the names of the last 10 people who worked on a document. This one is particularly dangerous because it's an automatic feature that you can't turn off. There's also no way to command Word to delete this information.

To get rid of this list of authors, you have to save the document in either RTF (Rich Text Format) or HTML and then resave it in Word. The problems are that it's an extra step most people won't take and it can be problematic because when you do this type of round-robin between formats, you get unpredictable results with formatting and other features.

Caution is Required

If you want to minimize the possibility of metadata causing a problem, the solution starts with an awareness. Remember that just because you can't see it, doesn't mean that it's not there.

Every good litigator is now aware of metadata and the general goldmine one can find in the digital versions of documents. If you find yourself in litigation, you should expect document requests to specifically ask for the digital version of documents and not a photocopy of a printout.

There are third party applications that purport to strip documents of their metadata and you may want to consider them. Still, you need to remember to run the metadata stripper with every version of the document you create. Moreover, you shouldn't assume that your stripper strips all the metadata. Be careful.

My best suggestion is to look to the developer of your software for information on the metadata their software collects. For example, Microsoft's Knowledgebase on their website is replete with information of their metadata. Read it or weep.

Chapter Eight

Privacy, Policy, and Encryption

IT'S ALL ABOUT PRIVACY

These days it's easy to become distracted. We're all doing our best to restart our stalling economy, while simultaneously managing our day-to-day affairs.

In the meantime, however, legislation is occurring around us that may affect the way your company conducts its business online. If you're not careful, while you're busy doing other things, your business might unknowingly violate some of these laws. For example, if either of the following two names sound familiar to you, raise your hand: The Gramm-Leach-Bliley Act, and the Health Insurance Portability and Accountability Act of 1996. These are just two of the many laws that have kicked into high gear over the past few months, either of which could seriously impact your online company.

Privacy is in many ways the No. 1 issue affecting the Internet. Unfortunately, from a legal perspective, it's still tough to tackle. We all want to do everything online, but we're not quite ready to give up all of our personal information or privacy rights to do it. We want the government to take a "hands-off" approach to governing the Internet, while at the same time we clamor for laws that punish those who steal our sensitive information using the ubiquitous resources of the Web.

Congress has tried to deal with online privacy through various pieces of legislation. From a business perspective, trying to keep tabs on Congress's love/hate relationship with e-privacy rules has driven more than one CEO to therapy. Although much of what is proposed never becomes law, some e-privacy rules have survived congressional roadblocks and presidential vetoes. The Gramm-Leach-Bliley Act is one such law.

Financial Privacy

Named after its congressional co-sponsors, the Gramm-Leach-Bliley Act (or GLB Act) requires companies that collect financial information, such as federal and state banks, financial brokers, and insurance brokers, to comply with strict guidelines concerning what they can (and can't) do with their clients' nonpublic financial information. The long arm of the GLB Act applies to all nonpublic financial information obtained by financial institutions about their customers, no matter how they got it.

This is a fancy way of saying that if you collect financial information about your clients, there's a good chance that your ability to share that information with other businesses is severely limited. Depending on the type of information you collect, you may have to obtain your clients' permission before sharing any of their financial information with your affiliates or any other third parties.

July 1 was the deadline for compliance with many of the GLB Act's privacy and security provisions. So, if you haven't checked in with your tech attorney in the past year or two, you might have blown right by the compliance deadlines without even realizing it. If you think you might be in violation of the Act, then run—don't walk—to your attorney's office. The penalties for noncompliance can be hundreds of thousands of dollars, or prison, or both.

Medical Privacy

The only thing we value more than our financial privacy is our medical privacy. After all, you'd probably rather have your stock portfolio disclosed than have some stranger discover that you have to apply an ointment to your "affected area" twice a day.

Enter the Health Insurance Portability and Accountability Act of 1996, or HIPAA. Originally designed to help employees with pre-existing medical conditions get into certain group health plans, HIPAA has evolved into a maze of e-privacy regulations that seeks to protect our medical records. Although it has been around since 1996, many of HIPAA's compliance deadlines are coming due within the next few years.

In short, HIPAA requires health plans, healthcare clearinghouses, and healthcare providers that conduct certain financial and administrative transactions electronically to adhere to certain strict privacy standards. These standards are designed to make sure that your medical information is used only for your own therapeutic purposes, and not to populate the mailing lists of third party drug providers, marketers, or other similar companies. Most immediately affected will be those insurance companies and medical billing companies that conduct part or all of their businesses online, or those companies that transmit patients' medical data to each other over the Internet.

In addition, as physicians move to Web-based billing systems or strive to achieve paperless offices, they too will become increasingly exposed to HIPAA's requirements.

The time is ripe to find out whether your e-business falls under HIPAA's privacy standards. Compliance deadlines are still far enough away to give you time to revamp the way you do things, but close enough to merit your attention sooner rather than later. Keep in mind that although the privacy deadlines are still a year or two away, like all deadlines you've ever faced, they'll be here before you know it.

As our lives become increasingly more complicated, it behooves us to remember that laws related to e-business are being passed and enforced all the time. Take a few minutes to think about how your e-business uses the data it collects, and consider whether your business might be running afoul of recent privacy legislation. If it is, or if you're not sure, then find out immediately and deal with it.

Online Privacy Issues

Online privacy is just a consumer and web surfer issue. Right? Actually, that's absolutely wrong. It's a major issue for your business. To the extent that your business has an online presence, you need to focus on online privacy issues to ensure that your customers and potential customers are happy campers who trust you with their private information.

In Europe, it's a fair generalization to say that they take privacy issues a bit more seriously than Americans do. They seem to see it as a fundamental human right akin to the way we see free speech. American companies doing business in Europe certainly need to be extremely sensitive to European sensibilities and laws relating to privacy.

In the United States, we give lots of lip service to privacy issues, but the fact is that there are few laws regulating privacy. While financial services and health care have laws that directly impact them, most businesses don't. Still, I think there's a certain inevitability to more privacy laws in the U.S.

I know that I have conflicting feelings on the issue. As a business lawyer, I want to help my clients maximize the value of the customer information they have without breaking the law or finding themselves on the front page of a newspaper with an article telling the world that they have "misused" personal information.

I put "misused" in quotes to help make the point that it's not just about "illegal" use. After all, there aren't many ways to break American privacy law because we have so little law to break. Still, "misuse" as I'm using it can simply mean "offend your customer's sensibilities." You always want to be a good guy when it comes to privacy.

I don't know about you, but if I bought a personal item at an online pharmacy, I wouldn't be too happy knowing that my buying habits were being bought and sold like pork bellies.

Ultimately, privacy begs for comprehensive Federal legislation. The thought of the Internet having 50 differing laws on privacy is a potential regulatory nightmare for companies who have an Internet presence. The costs of compliance could be astronomical and it might even be impossible depending on what these 50 laws say.

I would hate to see a day when websites have to exclude potential customers from certain states because they can't or won't comply with the privacy laws of that particular state.

For years, many of us who have followed legislative developments in this area have thought that Federal legislation was just around the corner. With the change in administrations, it now looks increasingly less likely.

In an environment where Congress won't act, states have historically taken the lead with legislation that sometimes becomes the model for Federal legislation if it works or a failed test that other states or Congress improve upon when they do act.

Minnesota (I will be good here and avoid all Governor Ventura jokes although it is a tempting target for at least some sarcasm) recently passed an interesting privacy law. As a state law, it only directly affects Minnesota, but it does increase the visibility of the privacy debate.

One of the things this new law regulates is what it calls "Personally identifiable information (PII)." PII includes things like physical and e-mail addresses, telephone numbers, what goods and services you may have bought, and the online sites you have visited. It provides some detailed rules about how this information can be used.

The law also regulates commercial e-mail, which is often called "spam." This new law does things like prohibit a false return address on an e-mail. Personally, I find it hard to conjure up an argument in favor of a false return address. It's sort of like favoring pollution.

The law also requires that spam include "ADV" as the first characters of the subject line. Further, if the material is of a sexual nature (I don't know about you, but I hate it when my kids get that junk), then the subject line must start with "ADV-adult." These subject line requirements will make it easy for filters to discard this junk before you even see it. It's the e-mail equivalent of throwing out all your "bulk rate" mail without opening the envelope.

There are common sense (let's not forget that "law" is "common sense" as modified by the courts and legislature) exceptions to the subject line

"ADV" rules. They include that the receiver consented to the message, and the sender and the receiver have a business or personal relationship.

One of the many interesting implications of a state law regulating the Internet is that businesses that aren't located in Minnesota may have to comply to the extent that they send e-mail into Minnesota. Now, what if you don't know where your receiver is located. After all, Joe8724@earthlink.net could be anywhere.

So, does that mean that you have to comply with Minnesota law for all your e-mail or risk penalties under Minnesota law? It's a good question without a clear answer. Someday, courts will provide answers to the many questions raised by this new law. Let the litigation begin.

THE CHILDREN'S ONLINE PRIVACY ACT: THE LAW AND ITS COMPLIANCE

If you control a website that collects personally identifiable information from children under the age of 13, you must ensure that your site complies with a relatively new Federal statute called the Children's Online Privacy Protection Act (COPPA) and rules enacted under COPPA. If you don't comply, you may find your company facing hefty penalties.

While there has been much talk about regulating online privacy in the United States, the reality is that the law doesn't impose many restrictions on the ways your business can use information it collects online from surfers. There are two recent prominent exceptions to this generalization.

The first covers financial services businesses like banks. If you're involved with financial services, you need to consider a new federal regulatory scheme, which deals with both online and offline privacy.

The second exception involves COPPA and children. If you're a website operator, COPPA regulates your online privacy policy, when and how you seek verifiable parental consent, and your responsibilities to protect children's privacy and safety online.

The first step in the compliance process is to determine if your site is directed to children. Refreshingly, the Federal Trade Commission uses a common-sense approach in its rules. It looks at the "[s]ubject matter, visual or audio content, the age of the models on the site, language, whether advertising on the web site is directed to children, information regarding the age of the actual or intended audience, and whether a site uses animated characters or other child-oriented features."

It is important to understand that COPPA applies to information, which you collect online, that would make a child individually identifiable. This information includes: full name, home address, e-mail address, and telephone number, and any other information that would allow the child's identity to be compromised or that would enable somebody to contact the child.

It also includes other types of information such as: hobbies, interests and information collected through cookies (no, not the kind of cookie you eat, but rather a small text file that your web browser saves on your hard drive; it might contain personally identifiable information), and other tracking mechanisms that may be linked to information that would disclose the child's identity.

Compliance

Let's be practical here. The easiest way to comply with COPPA is to not collect information from children under the age of 13. If young children aren't your target market (let's say you sell retirement plans), you should include a provision in your terms of website use that either prohibits children from using your site or at least warns them not to provide any personally identifiable information.

In case you're not familiar with terms of website use, it's the contract governing the use of your site by surfers. (You do have terms on your website, don't you?) Many sites just have a link at the bottom of their home page to the terms. Of course, we all know that nobody except first year law students (they read and analyze the back of laundry tickets, too) and people without a life (wink, wink) read them anyway.

Other sites make surfers click "I accept" to the terms before they can surf or buy things at their site.

Then, you should go a step farther. On the form where you might collect personally identifiable information, you might add a box asking the surfer to certify that they are not under the age of 13.

Of course, you'll have no way to really know that the surfer is telling the truth, but if you're not directly or indirectly gearing your site or a portion of your site to young kids, you'll probably be fine with these procedures in place.

Posting a Privacy Policy

If you do gear your site or a portion of it to kids under 13, you will have to give COPPA a close look. Among other things, you'll need to post a privacy policy. It must include specifics on the types of personal information you collect, how you'll use the information and whether the information will be passed on to advertisers or other third parties.

You have to give parents the right to agree to the collection and use of their child's information while also having the right to withhold consent from disclosures to third parties. You also have to give parents the right to access, review, and delete their child's information.

Parental Consent

The biggest headache with COPPA compliance is the requirement of parental consent. The consent must be actual (they gave the kid a computer, "that's consent" won't cut it here) and obtained using methods like e-mail and old fashioned snail mail. The method that you can use to get parental consent depends upon the way you will use the child's information.

If it's for internal purposes only, you can use e-mail. If you'll be disclosing the information to third parties, you'll need more meaningful consent, like a signature on paper or a fax.

To fully understand COPPA, you'd have to set up a flow chart with arrows going in different directions depending upon your answer to different questions. It's not that COPPA is conceptually complex, but still proper compliance requires attention to detail and can undoubtedly be expensive. You'll have to live with that because the blow to your reputation for non-compliance along with Federal Trade Commission penalties can be far more costly than compliance.

You need to be sensitive to the issues here. After all, we're dealing with children.

PRIVACY AND THE AMAZON.COM CASE

If you own an e-commerce or other type of online business, one of your most valuable assets is the information that you've collected about your customers. Like any business asset, you should use it to help you turn a profit. Caution is in order though unless you're willing to risk having the press mercilessly attacking you. Amazon.com just learned this lesson.

Some will tell you that the Net is like the "Wild West." While it's true in some ways, it's also true that in many ways everybody is watching the Net like a hawk.

While SallysDollShop.com can slide by in a relatively unregulated environment, if you manage a big name website like an Ebay.com or CNN.com, you're living under a microscope. One false step and the press jabs at you like you're a bull in a bullfight.

Even if you're a lower profile company, you're not off the hook. You still live in a world where negative publicity or even a disapproving customer buzz can cripple your bottom line.

The Amazon Tale

Of course, I've left many of you hanging since I mentioned that the press recently fried Amazon, but didn't tell you why. The "why" is that they changed their privacy policy in a way that made privacy advocates sizzle.

Here's the most controversial part (English translation follows). "As we continue to develop our business, we might sell or buy stores or assets. In such transactions, customer information generally is one of the transferred business assets. Also, in the unlikely event that Amazon.com, Inc., or substantially all of its assets are acquired, customer information will of course be one of the transferred assets."

Simply, this means that if Amazon sells some or all of its business or goes bankrupt, they can transfer whatever it is that they know about their customers to whomever ends up with their assets. So?

It's never been different. Businesses have been buying and selling business assets, including everything they know about their customers, since the first apple cart business changed hands in some place called the Garden of Eden.

Having said this, I should also point out that it's clearly not a PC (as in politically correct not personal computer) view. PC says that your privacy policy should say, "We treasure the trust that you have shown us by giving us your name, telephone number, and mailing and e-mail addresses. Under no circumstances will we ever reveal this information to anyone. Further, we'll never send you an unsolicited e-mail unless we first call you at home during dinner and ask you if that would be okay."

Why is it that PC seems to care less about that really annoying telephone call? Could it be that Net businesses get unfair scrutiny?

I'm a consumer too. I don't really want my name in a database along with a comprehensive list of everything I've bought in every drugstore, record store, and bookstore this year either.

Still, since the information is digital now and moves at Net speed, prohibiting its flow may be a bit like making it illegal for water to run downhill.

I'll go out on the not PC limb here. I think that what Amazon.com did was reasonable and responsible. Selling their customer list as a part of some future hypothetical sale of assets is just the way it has always worked and will always work.

Amazon.com isn't the evil one here. What they did was fully and frankly disclose a universal business practice.

Toysmart.com recently ran afoul on this issue when it tried to sell its customer list as a part of a sale of its assets. This, after it had a posted privacy policy that said, "When you register with Toysmart.com, you can rest assured that your information will never be shared with a third party." Selling information in the face of this explicit assurance is wrong. (I have my PC moments in this area.)

Post Your Privacy Policy

If you're responsible for a website that collects information about Web surfers, you should prominently post a privacy policy. It should include a clear disclosure of what information you collect, what you do with it, how you keep it secure, how customers can see the information you have, what choices they have about how you can use it, how they can fix incorrect information, and with whom you share the information.

The bad news is that the law is a bit unclear when it comes to where some of the lines are as to how you can legitimately use your customer's information. At the same time, this same uncertainty is the good news.

The political issue of what the law should be is an interesting question, but not the one your business needs to concern itself with today. For now, work with the broad parameters the law gives you and maximize the value of the information assets you possess. Furthermore, you should closely watch the law, and the outside parameters of PC, as they develop, so that you maximize your profit while not finding yourself at the ugly end of bad publicity.

He who walks the fine line just right can win this game as the rules quickly evolve.

E-SIGNATURES AND SAFETY

As businesses have increased the use of electronic records and contracts, one practical problem has been that you can't use a pen to sign a computer screen. (Well, technically you can sign the screen, but then you'd have to put the whole monitor in the file cabinet.) The good news for business is that now you have some legislation that will make it easier for you to use electronic signatures as a substitute for that quaint pen and ink John Hancock.

The idea of e-signatures as a substitute for traditional signatures isn't really a new idea at all. Several good technologies to implement e-signatures have been available for awhile.

The problem has been that while it made logical sense that an electronic record of a person's assent to an agreement should be valid, legal, and binding, the law hasn't necessarily been there to confirm the logic. While tech lawyers have generally been able to do a long-winded analysis that ended with "the e-signature was probably valid," "probably" is not always good enough. Would you do a million-dollar deal on a "probably?"

With the legislation, the answer is that an e-signature is as good as a pen and paper signature. The "probably" is gone.

The Law

In June 2000, Congress passed the Federal Electronic Signatures in Global and National Commerce Act (E-Sign). E-Sign creates two general rules.

The first is that "a signature, contract, or other record relating to such transaction may not be denied legal effect, validity, or enforceability solely because it is in electronic form." The second is that "a contract relating to such transaction may not be denied legal effect, validity, or enforceability solely because an electronic signature or electronic record was used in its formation." In plain English, the result of these two rules is that we now have a federal law that validates e-signatures.

Generally, E-Sign doesn't affect any requirement imposed by any other law. It's a narrow law that only deals with validating e-signatures. Importantly, what E-sign doesn't do is require any person to agree to use or accept electronic records or electronic signatures, other than a governmental agency in some cases.

Consumer Protection

As you might expect, consumers get some special protection under this new law. If a law requires that information be made available to a consumer in writing, the use of an electronic record to make it available is allowed only if the consumer has consented to receiving an e-notice and if the consumer, before consenting, was provided with a specific notice required by E-Sign.

The notice deals with things like any option to receive the information on paper, how to withdraw consent, and how to obtain a paper copy. One of the more interesting requirements is that a consumer must consent "electronically—in a manner that reasonably demonstrates that the consumer can access information in the electronic form that will be used to provide the information that is the subject of the consent."

This is a crucial consumer protection provision. It's designed to prevent a consumer from signing a paper form, which, in its fine print, has a consent to receive e-documents in a form that a consumer may not be able to read. If you're at all inclined to begin using electronic documents and contracts in your business, E-Sign is the most welcome thing to come your way in a long time. It's an open invitation to take your business methods into the 21st Century.

While this new Federal law is a big boost for e-signatures and e-documents, there's still a mix with state law that you need to closely examine.

My take on this is that it's now safe to rely on e-signatures in business. While there are more requirements when you're dealing with consumers than other businesses, you can even now do e-signatures with consumers. Just be sure that you're well-informed about the requirements of this new legal landscape before you jump in.

ENCRYPTION AND E-COMMERCE

Without encryption, e-commerce is nearly impossible. When you buy something online and use a "secure server," this means that your private information is being encrypted before it's sent over the Internet. Similarly, when you do Internet banking, your bank uses encryption to make your private financial information unreadable to anyone, but your bank.

"Encryption" is a set of complex mathematical formulae that permit anyone transmitting electronic information to scramble the message so that only the intended recipient can decode and thus understand it.

Encryption is essential for e-commerce because e-commerce largely takes place over the Internet, which is an open network. As a practical matter, this means that somebody other than the intended recipient of your information can intercept it and read it. Encryption protects your credit card number and all other private information you send.

There are several ways to learn whether your browser is encrypting your information. For example, when you purchase something online using Netscape's browser, if the picture of a lock in the lower left-hand corner is in the locked position with a glow around it, you're using encryption. You can also look at the Internet address of where your browser is. If it starts with "https" instead of just "http," it means that you're using a secure server that uses encryption.

The Inner Workings of Encryption

The basic concept of how you encrypt information is simple. You use a computer program, which uses an encryption algorithm (essentially a mathematical equation). This algorithm or equation converts the intended data (confidential files, credit card number, etc.) into an encoded message using a key (think of the "key" as your password for decoding or deciphering the message). The result of the encryption process is that your plain text message comes out the other end unreadable because it looks like gibberish.

Encryption comes in two basic flavors. One uses a single key (or password) and the other uses dual keys.

With single key encryption, you use the key to encode information, which you then send to your intended recipient. Your recipient then uses this same key to decipher the encrypted message. This means that you have to share the secret key with the recipient. The biggest problem with this is that you need a secure way to share the key. This limits the usefulness of single key encryption in E-commerce because it's rarely practical to whisper the key into someone's ear when you're doing business online.

Dual key encryption is the fuel of E-commerce. With this system, you have two mathematically related keys at work.

One key is called your "public key" and the other key is called your "private key." Your public key is a key that you can and should announce to the world. You can post it on your website and put it in an ad in the New York Times if you like. It's not a secret.

When somebody wants to send you a confidential message that only you should read, they encrypt it using your public key. If you want to send your credit card number to ReputableMerchant.com, your browser might encrypt it using ReputableMerchant.com's public key.

The interesting part of this is that if a thief intercepts your credit card number over the Internet and tries to decode it using ReputableMerchant.com's public key, it won't work. The beauty of a dual key system is that the public key is a one-way key. It encrypts information, but it won't decrypt it. That's why it's not important for you to keep it a secret.

When ReputableMerchant.com is ready to read your credit card number, its software will use ReputableMerchant.com's private key to decrypt or decode the information. The private key is the key that must remain absolutely secret. It's the one that lets somebody read messages intended only for them that were encrypted using their public key.

The Politics of Encryption

While strong encryption is essential for E-commerce, the United States government has traditionally been a world leader in encouraging encryption controls around the world. It has used economic and political pressure on other countries to encourage them to adopt restrictive policies. The problem is that while encryption is good for E-commerce, it's also good for criminals and espionage. After all, it's more difficult to convict a bookie of bookmaking if the books are encrypted.

Recently, the Electronic Privacy Information Center (www.epic.org) did a survey on encryption laws in other countries. In commenting on domestic controls, it said that, "Most countries do not restrict the domestic use of encryption by their citizens. Of the handful of countries around the world that do, few are democracies and most have strong authoritarian governments. The countries include Belarus, China, Israel, Kazakhstan, Pakistan, Russia, Singapore, Tunisia, Vietnam, and Venezuela. In many of those countries, the controls do not appear to be enforced."

In the United States, there aren't any restrictions on the manufacture, use, or sale of encryption technology within the country. We've treated exports quite differently.

Until the end of 1996, export of encryption technology was governed by the Arms Export Control Act, which was administered by the State Department. This meant that encryption software was considered a "munition." If you wanted to export it, the same laws that regulated nuclear missiles and tanks regulated you.

Since then, there has been a trend toward liberalizing those export restrictions. It's a trend that culminated in a recent White House announcement that said that export controls would be largely eliminated. The change will greatly simplify the Commerce Department's complex licensing requirements for the export of encryption software.

A ban on exporting encryption technology to terrorist countries like Iran, Iraq, Libya, Syria, Sudan, North Korea, and Cuba will remain.

This policy change finally recognizes that while we can limit export of strong encryption products from the United States, we can't change the fact that other countries already have strong encryption software. This policy only served to hurt American companies that couldn't compete in the global marketplace with others who had and could sell strong encryption software.

The Law Enforcement Perspective

In an attempt to balance this liberalization of export controls with the concerns of law enforcement, the White House also announced that it would support legislation to do several things to help the police cope with strong encryption.

The first step is committing $80 million over four years for a research center to help law enforcement agencies learn how to crack encryption.

This legislation would also create a legal framework that would allow the police to have access to "back-doors" under certain conditions. These "back-doors" are basically spare keys that the police can use to decode encrypted information. It goes without saying that the idea of a back door is especially controversial.

In addition, the proposed law would ensure that sensitive investigative techniques and industry trade secrets remain useful and secret by protecting them from forced disclosure in criminal and civil litigation. This essentially means that the police can decode your private information and not be compelled to explain how they did it. The alternative would appear to be that criminals would know too much about what code cracking capabilities the police had.

It all comes back to e-commerce requiring strong encryption. The Federal Government is finally getting this point and liberalizing its policies accordingly. Now we have to search for that fine balance between privacy and the need for the police to have access to proof of criminal activity. This debate is destined to go on for years.

Chapter Nine

Negotiations: Policies, Procedures, and Suggestions

THE ART OF NEGOTIATION: IMPROVING NEGOTIATING SKILLS ONLINE AND BEYOND

As a tech lawyer, the thing that I do more than anything else is negotiate. Almost every time I take a phone call or meet with somebody, I'm negotiating something. Most people are so unskilled at it that sometimes it feels like taking candy from a baby.

This chapter will be the first in an occasional series on improving your negotiating skills, which are central to tech deals and litigation, and every other type of business deal.

Getting Ready

It starts with preparation. Take the time to decide what you want and then chart a course for getting there. You rarely want to start by putting everything you need on the table. It's naive to think that there won't be give and take during the negotiating process.

You should also learn everything you can about the other side and the people representing the other side. The more you know about them, the more likely it is that you'll be able to satisfy their needs while taking care of your own.

In a complex negotiation, where you might have 100 or more points to hash out, you'll want to be sure to mix it up by discussing crucial points in between things you can give away. Resist the temptation to get the important stuff out of the way first.

In a negotiation, "information is power" is a cliché—and it's also absolutely true. Strategic information (in fact, any information) is something you should only give away parsimoniously and then only when you get some information back as a quid pro quo.

Sometimes I'll start a negotiation by saying, "Let's get the stuff that's really important to you first." It's often a good tactic because I'm making them feel loved while getting them to give me crucial information about their big issues. It's likely that until they were done telling me about the "important stuff," I didn't have an accurate picture of their agenda.

With this true picture of their big issues, the game begins. With these crucial issues identified, I now know the areas I'll have to give the most on. That's fine, but I'm going to make them stomach the things that are important to me in return for giving them what's important to them. Or maybe I won't.

I might keep them off balance by linking my little issues up to their big issues. If I do it this way, when that round is over, I've now given on issues I had to give on anyway and scored on lots of smaller issues.

What is now left are my big issues. With some dancing, I might be able to win on those points without having to give too much back—because other items that they might hope to trade off on were already put to bed earlier in the negotiation.

While this may be a legitimate example of how a negotiation might proceed, it's also a gross oversimplification of the dynamic of a complex business negotiation. For one thing, when there are a hundred points on the table, a skilled negotiator never falls into the trap of agreeing that he can never revisit earlier points.

You shouldn't visualize your negotiation as a linear progression from one point to the next. Rather, it's arrows pointed in all directions linking points in the most unexpected ways. If you have to give on a particular point, then push back on something, maybe even something you had given on earlier. Never give without getting something back.

Be Quiet

People love to hear themselves talk, but a skillful negotiator listens. When you walk into that conference room to negotiate your big deal, or take that phone call to discuss your little deal, you already know what it is that you want. It's not important to make sure that the other side instantly knows that. What's important is that you learn their agenda and their needs. You've got to get inside their heads, and this requires listening.

Early in a negotiating session, you should ask open-ended questions and just listen. If you want to interrupt, don't. Let them talk. The more you listen, the more you learn.

I can't overemphasize this point enough. As we walk into a conference room, I'll often remind my client to listen. He assures me that he will listen. Then, no sooner are we done shaking hands and talking about the weather and my client won't shut up. Get the Pepto Bismol. He's got diarrhea of the mouth.

It's like a manager telling a boxer, "Jab, jab, jab." No sooner does the bell ring and he's out there flailing wildly.

You've got to take the game plan into the game. Write yourself a note if you have to. "Listen! Don't talk. Never interrupt."

As you work on improving your negotiating skills, remember that it begins with preparing, developing a game plan, listening a whole lot, and talking very little. If you can just start with that, you'll be a much-improved negotiator.

MORE ON THE ART OF NEGOTIATION

Let's continue with the situation where you need something in a deal that you know will give the other side heartburn. Let's say you're a smaller software developer who creates custom software with a hefty price tag. Normally, you give your customers onsite service with a fast response time. In fact, central to your reputation in the industry is your reputation for support. Of course, you're able to do what you do by selling only within 100 miles of your office.

Now, you're discussing selling your product to a company that's 3,000 miles away.

You want the sale, but to do it you're going to have to sell the other side on the "outrageous" (from their perspective) idea that you'll provide support by telephone and by tying into their system remotely. What is one to do?

Sometimes the answer is to drop the idea early, let them vent about how outrageous the thought is, and then move along to other issues, promising to resolve this one later.

This often works because time works wonders. The idea is that if you're going to propose an outrageous idea, do it early in the negotiations and then move on. It's an amazing thing but my experience has been that the mere passage of time helps it go down better than last week's tuna fish.

I think it has something to do with "precedent." The problem with your idea was that it was unprecedented. You're known for your incredible response times with a live body and now you're suggesting (drum roll please) "telephone tech support only."

A month later, as you're progressing toward the final details of your deal, a funny thing will have happened with the concept of telephone tech support.

It will no longer be a new and unprecedented idea. It will be an idea that they've heard before, albeit from you, but still it's no longer a new idea. The result is that the idea will often be more palatable.

It's ironic that time can have this magical power. Then again, when you consider the magical power time can have in helping us cope with whatever it is that life throws at us, this use of the "mere passage of time" and the dramatic results I'm suggesting you can get as a negotiator, seem trivial.

This is an example of why you can't usually effectively compress negotiations into an arbitrarily short time. Time itself is a part of the process. If you ignore this truism, you may risk a poor result.

The Nibble

The flip side of dropping a bombshell on the other side early is nibbling late. The more time, effort, and money the other side invests in you, the more they want and need to do the deal with you. Nobody wants to spend weeks working a deal and lose it right at the end.

Drop the big ones early, but then you should save some little stuff for some nibbles at the end. Let's say you're buying 1,000 desktop computers for your company and they're proposing 20-gigabyte hard drives. You know you need at least 30 gigs.

If you bring this issue to the fore early, you're likely to find yourself paying "retail" for the difference in cost. Mention it when your pen is about a millimeter from the paper and you may find that they'll just give you the bigger hard drives at their wholesale cost. (Nibbles are often delivered with that innocuous, "Oh, by the way" lead in like "Oh, by the way, it turns out we really need 30-gig hard drives and I can't spend more than this.")

I will say this about nibbling. While it's often effective, you win few friends doing it. I don't recommend it when you intend an ongoing relationship, but it may fit your needs when negotiating a one-time deal.

It Can Be Win-Win

In a negotiation, you should never lose sight of the fact that you're usually negotiating more than money. If it will be a long-term deal, you should never forget that you need to live with these people long after you sign the contract. A nibble, although a time-honored and legitimate tactic, is probably not one you should use as you finish negotiating an employment contract.

Then again, it might be a perfect way to get something like that long-planned family vacation, which will happen to fall one month after you start, although the normal policy is no vacations for the first six months.

The overriding point is that negotiation isn't war or litigation (government-sanctioned legalized warfare). It's a process that should end in a deal that's a compromise of everybody's initial positions. Give and you'll get. Avoid words like, "This is a deal point" or "This is not negotiable."

Speak softly. State your points gently. When the other side raises the pitch, you lower it.

Remember that negotiating isn't a science. Rather, it's an art honed by experience. Still, by studying this art and learning for the experience of others, you'll improve faster.

MORE NEGOTIATING POWER

Whether it's a tech deal, a lawsuit or any other type of business deal, you're going to need to bring the same negotiating skills to the table.

Telephone Talks

Negotiating a deal by telephone is practical and can be effective for simple deals that aren't important to you. As for complex and important matters, my advice on negotiating by telephone is simple and easy: Don't. I'm hard pressed to imagine anything less effective than lots of amorphous voices on a speakerphone trying to negotiate a complex deal. It's slow. It's ponderous. Moreover, it's ineffective.

The upsides of the telephone are probably limited to two. One is that it's easier to arrange a telephone call than a meeting. The second is that you save money by negotiating by telephone rather than in person. While the first one is undoubtedly true, the second one may be an illusion. While you may save on the front end by reducing your travel expenses, you may cost yourself money in the long run.

The problem with the telephone starts with losing all your visual cues. You can't see the other person's body language or eyes. If you're good at reading people, those signs can be more important than what they say. I also find that it's easier for people to say "no" and be obstinate on the phone. Maybe that flows from the distance the telephone brings. There's just something about looking somebody in the eyes that brings people together.

The telephone also fosters less focus. If you call a meeting, you monopolize everyone's attention. This usually helps to move the deal. The advantages of this focus may even offset the additional time that it may take to organize a meeting.

Yet another problem with the telephone is that you lose the ability to have back-channel communication. When I'm sitting next to my client, it's easy to write notes or simply walk out of the room for a private discussion. On the telephone, people seem to forget about how important that back channel can be.

This one can be easier to overcome than some of the other problems with telephone negotiations. Sometimes I'll suggest that my team run AOL's Instant Messenger while we're on the conference call, so that we can type back-channel messages to each other. It's nice to be able to quickly type, "Don't go in that direction," or "Be quiet. I think they're about to give on that point."

Your cellphone can also be a good tool to help overcome the back-channel problem. It can be as easy as walking out of the room and using it to privately discuss a point.

No Authority

Ever notice that when you buy a car, the "sales manager" with the authority to make the deal is invisible in some ivory tower. You talk to the salesman, who is always on your side (sort of like a pet rattlesnake) and is on the edge of being fired for giving you such a great deal. The problem is that he can't make the deal. He can only "propose" the deal to the invisible sales manager, who always says no, as they slowly drive up the price in successive rounds of this charade.

Not bringing the decision maker to the table is a monstrously effective technique. Large tech companies like IBM, Computer Associates, and Microsoft do it all the time. You bring your president and lawyer to the table to get the deal done, and they send a salesperson and paralegal. You make concessions and they take things to the ivory tower and get back to you because they don't have authority.

Don't fall into the trap of bringing too much authority to the table. Never ever have more authority on your side of the table than the other side has. If they send a mid-level person, you send a mid-level person. When things are going too slow, if they want the deal, they'll suggest that the decisionmakers meet. If they never make that suggestion, it tells you something about the importance they place on your deal.

The problem with an imbalance of power is that no authority creates a situation where a person can't give away the tough points. This leaves it to the side that brought a decisionmaker to the table to give away important points as both sides push to close the deal.

Set your ground rules before the "big meeting" (or phone call—if you must). Make sure that you know who will participate and what authority they have. Then make sure that your side has the same or less authority than the other side.

As for the next time you buy a car, my advice is when you get down to the nitty-gritty, you let your kid discuss price and walk their offers to you, while you sit in the car. When they get tired of your farce, the guy in the ivory tower will make his royal appearance. Then, it's time to cut the deal.

NEGOTIATING TECH DEALS

Tech related deals sometimes lead to disputes just like any other type of agreement. It might be a software development deal gone sour, an outsourcing deal straight from hell or whatever, but things go wrong. When they do, lawsuits often follow. This is your "how to" on negotiating your way out of a major dispute involving technology.

Let's start with the end and work our way forward. I'm often asked why it is that disputes tend to settle only as the trial approaches. It turns out to be a complex question that defies a simple answer.

Part of it is that the parties use the discovery process (things like depositions and subpoenas) to learn about the other's strength and weaknesses. This takes time and delays the time when the parties are ready to talk.

Another issue is the purely emotional side. A lawsuit is essentially "civilized" society's way of handling warfare between its members. (I put "civilized" in quotes because having participated in hundreds of hearings, I've watched many a lawyer act in a way that defies my definition of civilized.) Lawsuits are ritualized, expensive, and complex, and sometimes I think not an improvement over trial by ordeal. Part of the ceremony is that people yearn to vent before they want to talk. It's all too human.

Yet another part of the answer is the lawyers. Now, don't get me wrong. Pure litigators are an important part of the legal profession, but so are soldiers. We need them both and they serve a purpose.

Still, you won't find too many soldiers who make great diplomats. It's a different personality type. If you want to negotiate early and seriously, I would suggest to you that the litigator is not the lawyer you want taking the lead.

Life is like that. You go to Midas Muffler and you usually walk away with a muffler. You see a surgeon and you usually walk (or roll) away with stitches. See a litigator and guess what, you're likely to end up involved in a lawsuit.

It's not an evil conspiracy to clog the courts. It's just a mindset. Warriors fight wars. Diplomats negotiate treaties.

If I were the client, I would ask my litigator which lawyer in the firm is the best deal negotiator. Rarely is that someone in the litigation department. I would politely (honey is usually better than vinegar) ask to bring that person in to consult on negotiating a settlement.

If you have a tech dispute, you want the person who is best at doing complex tech deals. Have him evaluate your situation. Then, ask your lawyers to two-track your case. What I'm suggesting with the "two-track" is that you simultaneously litigate and work on negotiating at the same time.

Too often, lawyers handle lawsuits sequentially. The traditional sequence starts with a token effort at resolution. I say token because all too often it consists of a nasty letter that ends with "Please be governed accordingly." In my book, that's not exactly the language of diplomacy.

Then comes the token settlement meeting or worse the quick call, which represents one last effort to settle. Next, somebody declares war. At this point, the lawsuit develops a life of its own.

As the client, you need to try to short-circuit the "life of its own part." Show strength through your litigator, but I strongly suggest a vigorous effort to settle simultaneously.

The strongest objection that people will have to this advice is that by showing a willingness to negotiate early, you're telling the other side that you think your case is weak. It sounds good, but I find that in the fog of litigation (like war), the other side really can't get anything out of your willingness to negotiate. If fact, the ironic part is that they may be just as willing as you are to negotiate, but don't have the skill or strategic sense to know how to make it happen.

When you get them to the negotiating table, you should not expect the process to be easy. After all, you're at war with them. Expect them to vent. And, you should vent too, but let them go first.

In any negotiation, I'm a big advocate for listening early and talking later. Remember that in the first hours of your negotiation, it's more important for you to know their position. You'll tell them yours in good time. Be a good listener, be willing to compromise (although you feel that you shouldn't have to compromise), and you may just find your lawsuit behind you. It's usually good business.

NEGOTIATIONS FOR
WEBSITE DEVELOPMENT

It's a nightmare scenario. You're in charge of your company's major website redesign project and the site is horrendous. Even your mother hates it. As you consider where to mail your resume, you might want to consider what you'd do differently next time.

Tech projects fail for many complex reasons. I've litigated those fiascoes.

One recurring theme is communication failure, which easily occurs when you have techies, business people, bean counters, and lawyers in one room pretending to speak the same language.

Techies understand what they can build. Business people know what they want for their customers. Bean counters want it to be close to free, and the lawyers—what exactly is it that we do and why are we in the room anyway?

I've asked that question many times when I've lectured. The answers I get make it clear that people love lawyers. One of the common answers is "so that we can write a contract that will let you sue the other side if they don't do what they said they would do." While that's true, it's like saying you build a jet so that you can play with the ejection seat.

The lawyer is there to foster communication. You write a contract to prevent litigation.

Using a website development agreement as an example, you must ensure that your agreement clearly defines who will do what, when, how, how much it will cost, and who will own whatever it is that you create. Few form contracts come close to meeting this standard.

One area that often raises red flags is the issue of who owns the intellectual property in the completed website. The buyer's perspective is "we paid for it, we own it." The seller's view is that there are reusable things built into your site that the buyer can't own.

This is a problematic area where each side is partially right. As a buyer, you shouldn't expect to own everything.

It's rarely framed as a price issue, but the negotiation is often facilitated if it is. A smart developer doesn't say, "You can't own the copyright." Rather, she says, "you can own it, but since I can't reuse it, you'll have to pay me more."

Buyers of web development services should consider what they really need to own versus what they need a license to use. They may need to own the look and any secret sauce that gives them a distinct advantage over their competitors.

By the way, the general rule is that to the extent your agreement is silent on who owns the intellectual property, the developer owns it. That's counterintuitive, since the buyer paid for it, but it's a mistake people easily make in tech contracting.

Another area to focus on is the "standard" limitation of liability. Most website development agreements have a clause which, when reduced to its essence, says, "No matter what we do and no matter how bad it is, we owe you very little money and you owe us your first-born."

These types of clauses have become the norm, but that doesn't mean that there isn't room for negotiation.

For example, if the clause limits you to a refund of what you paid, you might ask that the limit of liability be increased to the total you will pay during the entire life of the contract.

Imagine making a small first payment of $100,000 on a much larger contract, watching your developer screw-up the project, losing business due to the screw-ups, and then finding out that all you get for "damages" is a refund. It's not right and you should push for more.

You should also ask to exclude liability to third parties. If you don't and you're sued because the developer created a website that infringed somebody's copyright, you may have no recourse against your developer.

Last, but not least, is that the limitations of liability should be reciprocal. What's good for them is good for you. Why should the developer have a limit of liability and not you? The answer is that you should have one too.

TIPS ON NEGOTIATING TECH DEALS

Businesses buy technology-related goods and services all the time. Just to name a few examples, they buy the services needed to create a sophisticated e-commerce website, custom develop software, and generally provide technology solutions for their business. The way the parties usually handle the paperwork is that the vendor gives the customer their form and the customer signs it. After all, the form is printed so it can't be changed. Wrong!

I have two comments about those forms. One, I represent vendors as well as buyers of these services. Trust me when I tell you that if you're the customer, you never want to accept those form contracts without changes.

They're designed to be one-sided in favor of the vendor. I write them. I know.

Secondly, they're almost always negotiable. The basic premise is that most customers won't read them carefully and even fewer will take the time to really negotiate them. A smart customer sees the form as nothing more than a one-sided first offer and goes from there.

Involve a Lawyer?

Clearly, you can't involve a computer lawyer every time you buy something computer-related. So, how do you know when you need legal assistance?

I think that you make that judgement based on what's at stake. You have to look at the size of the contract and the importance of whatever it is that you're buying. Essentially, I'm suggesting a quick, down and dirty cost-benefit analysis.

I recommend that you start by assuming that the form contract you're seeing was written by a skilled lawyer whose marching orders were to write a contract that gives you as little protection as possible. Next, imagine that the deal goes badly. The final step in this analysis is to assume that if you're forced to sue under the contract, you'll lose because the form agreement had a pro-vendor bias.

How much would you lose? How bad would this scenario damage you? If the damage is more than what is an acceptable loss to you, then you need a lawyer on your side too.

A problem in doing this cost-benefit analysis is that you may not know everything that you need to know to make these judgments. In that case, I suggest consulting with a lawyer to help you with your cost-benefit analysis.

Some Red Flags—Damage Limitations

One of the things you should always focus on is damage limitations. Be leery of clauses like, "Vendor's liability for any loss, damage or expense of any kind, resulting from the products or services, negligence, or any other cause whatsoever, regardless of the form of action, whether in tort or in contract, shall be limited to the selling price of the products or services." Variations on this type of clause may limit you to six months of service charges or some predetermined, and usually low, dollar figure.

Reduced to its essence, this clause says that no matter what they do to you, the most you get is a refund. So, you pay them lots of money to redo your office network, the system functions poorly, you lose lots of money, and you get—a refund. It's not fair, but if you sign a contract with a damage limitation, you may have to live with it.

I say "may" because some courts, in some contexts, won't enforce contracts that are too onerous. Still, in negotiating a contract, you certainly don't want to agree to a damage limitation in the hopes that if it ever mattered, a court won't enforce it.

Some states prohibit disclaimers of responsibility for negligence in some types of contracts. The more general rule is that a party can limit its liability for ordinary negligence, but not gross negligence.

Gross negligence is a difficult concept to define since it lacks a bright-line test. Generally, the concept is that "gross negligence" entails conduct that's almost willful and something worse than just ordinary negligence.

Limitations of Time to Sue

Many agreements have provisions like "No action, regardless of form, arising out of or related to this agreement may be brought by the customer more than one year after a cause of action has arisen." This clause and similar ones reduce the time that the law gives you to file a lawsuit.

For example, most states will give you four or five years to file a breach of contract claim. This clause, which you should assume is enforceable, reduces you to one year.

In my experience, this is a perfect example of a clause that's always negotiable. It's as simple as you taking the time to focus on it and asking for something better. I'd start by asking that the clause be deleted as unnecessary. The law provides for a statute of limitations and your lawyer should argue that it's not needed. Even if they say no to that, they always agree to something more than the printed language. Even if you agree to three years instead of one, you've come out better.

Is this significant? I can't know that without a crystal ball. I'd have to know if a situation will ever arise where you'd need or want extra time to file a lawsuit or make a claim.

The point is that you often don't know whether what you do when you negotiate a contract will matter. When you're negotiating, you're often just dealing with possibilities. Sometimes you have to wait until the contract plays itself out to know whether it mattered.

I don't think that the question, "Is it significant?" is the right question. Yet, that's the one people ask. It's as if by some magic the FORM becomes the starting point of what's significant and fair.

Don't let the vendor's form take on magical properties. It's nothing more than their idea of what a one-sided deal should look like. I can assure you that if I ignored the vendor's form and created a pro-customer contract from scratch, it would be completely different from the vendor's.

My pro-customer contract wouldn't even mention statute of limitations and if it did, I'd say five years instead of one. Usually, I'd be happy to live with the law's typical four or five-year period. Look at how different the whole dynamic of the negotiation changes if it's my form and the vendor is now "asking" that we reduce it to one year. It seems so unfair. Moreover, "fairness" not "significance" should be your primary focus in a negotiation.

In negotiating your agreements, you must avoid that very natural tendency to see the deal's starting point as being the vendor's form. You should first see the deal from your one-sided perspective. What do you want and need?

In a negotiation, you're not likely to get everything you want either, but you must work to pull contracts back to the middle, i.e., back to what's fair.

You shouldn't ask for changes in a vendor's form only after asking yourself whether the change is significant. If it's one sided in favor of the vendor, ask that the provision be made neutral.

If the vendor asks that you indemnify them for your wrongdoing, you should ask that they indemnify you for their wrongdoing. If they get attorney's fees if they're the prevailing party, then you should if you're the prevailing party. If they can terminate the agreement if you sell your company, the reverse should be true.

After you've put every unfair provision on the table, you can use the issue of "significance" to decide which points to give up. Certainly, not every point has equal importance to you.

Just remember, what's good for them is good for you. That's fairness.

Don't walk into a deal thinking about how big they are. They want your business or they wouldn't be talking to you. Sure, the Microsofts of the world budge less than the local vendor down the road, but they all bend. The only way to find out how far is to push back.

NEGOTIATING AS A TEAM

If you ever saw the movie The Godfather, you may remember a scene where the Godfather's family is negotiating getting into the illegal narcotics business with another family.

The Godfather is adamantly opposed to selling drugs. His son though (played by James Caan) chimes in over his father and says that maybe pop is wrong.

Jump to the next scene and you have a furious pop telling his son to never ever disagree with him in public again. To the outside world, they're one family with one position.

Jump ahead a few more scenes and you see an attempted assassination of the Godfather. Later we learn that the motive behind the assassination was to make James Caan the family's leader because he was willing to enter the drug trade.

The Godfather had it right. If you want to be effective in your negotiations, your team must have a single unified voice. Show disharmony to the other side, and if they're any good, they'll use it to shear holes right through you.

You start hearing things like, "Your lawyer said that this is a non-negotiable deal point, but you're saying it isn't." Don't ever do that to me or any member of your negotiating team.

Don't forget the five Ps: Prior Planning Prevents Poor Performance.

Before you begin negotiations, spend time planning your positions. Going in, you should know things like what you need and want, what your bottom-line positions will be, and where you'll start.

You should also choreograph who's your lead speaker and who's playing backup to reinforce points. Also, you should agree not to hesitate to leave the room together to privately discuss any internal points of disagreement as they come up during the negotiation.

Coming back to my Godfather story, the Godfather's rule is a cardinal one. Speaking now from the perspective of outside counsel who is often hired in the role of professional negotiator, and frankly usually paid quite well for the role, once my client has disagreed with me in public, I might as well go home. He's now told the other side that a back channel around me might get them a better deal.

It's a simple rule and don't ever break it. No member of the negotiating team should ever publicly disagree with another member. Period. Do it and you're an amateur waiting to be eaten alive.

Once I notice internal discord on the other side, I look for ways to have back-channel communication with the guy whose position is most favorable to my client. My goal is to make him an ally and then let him sell it to his side. Cliché time—"Divide and conquer."

Let's say we're buying a software company and the biggest advocate for the deal on the other side is their director of marketing. I'll go out of my way to privately let him know that we think the marketing department is one of his company's strengths and budget won't be an issue under the new regime. You get the picture. It has something to do with saliva dripping from his mouth.

I remember one client in particular (and this was years ago) who just didn't get it when I talked about a united front. We were just acquiring a division of a company. The problem was that one of the human beings on the other side had the personality of a rabid dog on a bad day.

This was a complex negotiation that went on for days. We would start each day with a private meeting. We'd agree on what positions the client wanted to take. I'd reiterate that we can and should evolve our positions during the course of the day as things develop, but we should do it in a unified way after a private discussion in the hallway (be careful about who might be sitting on the other side of that cubicle wall).

After all, in a negotiation your position must evolve. Here's the caveat though. Whoever took the position that you're changing should be the one to deliver the message about the compromise position.

You emasculate your lawyer, acting in his role of professional negotiator, when you publicly modify the position he took for you. In the deal with my friend the rabid dog, I finally resigned. The client was simply incapable of effectively using a professional negotiator.

It's frustrating to privately discuss a strategy and as soon as the game begins watch a person with no stomach for the stress of a sophisticated business negotiation give it all away. They wore him out. He felt desperate to do the deal, they knew it, they played tough, and he caved in faster than a house of cards. I felt like I was coaching a little league team against the New York Yankees.

The close for this chapter is simple. Remember the story about the Godfather.

OUTSOURCING BUSINESS TECHNOLOGY

If your technology company is like most (or if you're not a tech company, but use a lot of technology in your business), you've probably considered outsourcing technology as an effective, cost-cutting measure. How you begin the process of deciding to outsource can be just as important as the decision to outsource itself. To that end, a good exploratory team can mean the difference between enjoying a successful outsourcing endeavor and enduring a recurring corporate nightmare.

Without a doubt, one key to successful outsourcing is deciding which area of your business you want (or need) to outsource. It's not easy and you shouldn't do this yourself. It's virtually impossible for you to know every aspect of your business, and be fully informed about which of your departments or internal business functions are ripe for outsourcing.

Building a Team

First create an exploratory team, and let the team conduct the initial investigation into the advantages and disadvantages of outsourcing a particular function.

Building an exploratory team is different from simply gathering your colleagues and setting an agenda. In a perfect world, you'd approach your colleagues and ask, "Hey, who wants to help me figure out a way to outsource some of our business functions and save this company some money?" Everyone would joyfully accept your offer, and the world would be a peaceful, happy place. But, let's get back to reality.

If your company is like most, many of your employees will give you every conceivable excuse not to outsource. I predict that shortly after you make your request for volunteers, your e-mail inbox will begin to fill with messages like, "We don't need to outsource," or "Our work is too important to out-source."

Don't be discouraged when this happens. It's entirely understandable and completely predictable. After all, you may think you're saying the word "out-source," but what your employees really hear is "You're fired," or "We're looking into ways to get rid of you." To them, outsourcing is akin to supply-ing them with a company shovel and asking them to dig their own corporate graves. In other words, you should expect the team selection process to be a bit rocky.

Choosing a Leader

To begin, pick a team leader. The leader will be responsible for setting the tempo and direction of the team, and serve as the team's mouthpiece as well. It makes sense, therefore, to pick a leader who shares your vision and objec-tive of outsourcing. Of course, this is easier said than done, because even the candidates for team leader might fear losing their jobs to outsourcers. In fact, it's often said that for a team leader to seriously (and impartially) consider outsourcing, she should be at least two levels above the area you're consider-ing outsourcing. Once you've selected the team leader, you have to begin staffing your team with competent employees who understand the long and short-term goals of your company. Many companies limit membership of the team to supervisors and upper-level managers—this is a big mistake. Clearly, you'll need the input of upper-level management, because they're in the best position to analyze high-level issues and provide guidance in areas to which most employees are not regularly exposed. However, low-level employees can help the process too.

First, they often understand the day-to-day needs of your employees better than your managers. Second, by including them, your team will appear bal-anced and fair, instead of elitist and unresponsive. In any event, your goal should be to create a team that represents a cross section of your company.

Outside Advisors

Without question, your team should also include outside advisors, such as your company's attorney and accountant. Outside advisors can increase the efficiency of your team by providing objective advice, and making sure that the team's goals remain within the boundaries of practicality. Also, advisors can even the playing field when it comes time to draft and review requests for proposal, or negotiate outsourcing contracts. Often it's easier (and cheaper, I know) to include advisors at the initial decision-making level, rather than bring them in after the team has drawn its conclusions or, worse, has become deadlocked.

Further, if your tech lawyer brings legitimate experience in negotiating outsourcing agreements to the table, the earlier you involve him, the better. Early, he can do more to guide and nudge your deal in the direction you'll want it to ultimately go. Later, agendas are set and the outline of the deal is established. Moving the deal in a material way after the parties have developed expectations is harder and in some cases may be impossible.

Bear in mind that your experience base in negotiating outsourcing deals may be small, but hopefully your tech lawyer has been there and done this before. Everybody makes more mistakes when their experience level is low. In these situations, it's usually wise to hire a professional to set the course in unfamiliar territory.

Picking an exploratory team and negotiating your deal isn't necessarily fun or easy. You'll have to make some hard decisions and, at least temporarily, you'll likely be the target of company paranoia, strife, and criticism. Nonetheless, there is no better way to explore the advantages you may reap from outsourcing than to pick the right team and forge ahead.

TIPS FOR TECH PURCHASES

If you're currently in the market for technology purchases, here are some tips that can help you ensure that you get the most for your money.

Vendor Forms

You should always assume that a form contract is completely negotiable. While this may not always be true for small deals, once you're spending real money, you should presume that the form they've presented you is merely their first offer.

The typical scenario is that their sales folks talk to you about a few high level points. They'll tell you what they can create, how wonderful it will be, how it will pay for itself before you've even paid them, and on and on it goes. The "details" that get discussed are often not much deeper than price, delivery date, and functionality.

Then comes this monster agreement filled with details nobody discussed. It never ceases to amaze me how even sophisticated business folks treat that document with reverence. It's nothing more than their lawyer's one-sided take on what the deal should be.

As someone who drafts these contracts for vendors, trust me when I tell you that I write them assuming that there will be some push back from the other side. If you don't push back, well, let's just say that you're making a big mistake. Furthermore, if you don't get help from a lawyer with lots of legitimate experience doing these types of deals, you're at a tactical disadvantage and you will end up on the losing end of this negotiation.

The Basic Business Points

At some level, the agreement should correctly and clearly state the business points that you actually discussed with them. Is the price as discussed? Did the understanding on features make its way from the salesperson's mouth to your contract? If not, don't expect the features because when it's not there, "But the salesperson said so," will be a losing plea.

It's so elementary, but you must be sure that everything you were promised makes its way to the contract. Don't be so foolish as to accept, "Don't worry. The contract is just a formality. We'll do it like we promised." Of course, it's that sort of foolishness that keeps my litigation plate full.

The Undiscussed Part

Before the first draft of the contract appears, few business people fully discuss issues like limitations of liability, warranty, indemnification, and other similar issues. Business folks tend to relegate these and similar issues to the world of "lawyer's points." You can label them whatever you want, but they are important. Get it wrong on some of the "lawyer points" and you may find yourself without a meaningful remedy if your deal doesn't pan out as you might have hoped.

Not surprisingly, most form contracts presented by vendors have a vendor-favorable take on these "lawyer points." You can always do better if you take the time to professionally negotiate your deal.

It's your money. Why should you be promised the world by a salesperson, but your agreement says that you accept whatever it is they deliver to you "as is." That's not a warranty, folks. Why is it that the agreement limits their liability to you in case of a dispute to whatever it is you paid them. In plain English, that means that no matter what they do to you and no matter how bad it is, the most you get is a refund. Moreover, why is it that they get a limitation of liability, but you don't?

A typical vendor provided form agreement has pages and pages of one-sided protection for the vendor. I'll typically negotiate to either remove these provisions or make them apply to both parties. The old cliché should apply: What's good for the goose, is good for the gander.

It Takes Time

One of the things vendors count on during negotiations is that the buyer is more anxious to consummate the deal than they are. Car dealers depend on the same thing to put you at a disadvantage during negotiations. Don't fall into the trap.

You must clearly communicate to your vendor that you're not in a rush to sign anything. You'll sign when the contract is right and not one minute before. Just that small bit of posturing can help level the playing field.

Any smart negotiator will use time against you if he can. Don't fall victim to it.

Then you need to manage your own expectations. Technology deals simply take time to properly document in a contract. The deals tend to be complex and there is no magical one-size-fits-all form.

KEEP TECH LAWYER ON COMPANY TEAM

You signed your big deal. Next, you pop the corks, thank your tech lawyer for his great work, and send him home. The legal part is mercifully over and now you can get back to business sans lawyers. Sorry, but it's the wrong approach in tech deals, and in fact, in any big deal of any kind. You must keep the team intact and functioning.

Once you sign your agreement, you should begin the process of managing the deal. If you don't manage it, then your vendor will. I would point out that it should be obvious that you may not have overlapping priorities.

It doesn't matter if the deal was custom software modification, implementing a new network for your company, an overhaul of your website, or whatever. If you manage the project right, you'll maximize the value of whatever it is you bought.

You took the time to put together a team to decide what it is you needed, you evaluated several companies, and you spent time negotiating your deal. One common mistake I see all the time is that at this point many businesses dismantle the deal team because it's "done."

Well, as Yogi Berra said (and if he didn't say it, he should of), "It ain't over til it's over." Don't dismantle the team!

There's no one-size-fits-all formula here, but the idea I'm floating is that your team must stay together throughout the implementation phase. You might need a weekly meeting or just a monthly conference call among your team members, but whatever, you need to manage the process.

You want your team to give you input on issues like "are you getting the service levels required by your agreement?" Are you receiving the required status reports from your vendor? Are they meeting deadlines? In the broadest sense, you want to know if your vendor is complying with the terms of the agreement.

All too often, I see many companies not doing as I suggest here. Rather, they deal with issues like this through crisis management. They tend to be reactive instead of proactive. Only when the situation gets ugly do they reassemble the team and try to reel the vendor back in.

I know that in my role as outside counsel, some of my clients don't take this advice. Once the corks pop, I'm out of it unless and until the parties are staring down the barrel of a rifle. Then, I'm asked to fix it before there's a war.

It should be obvious that it's much harder to fix a problem than prevent it. If your vendor's performance isn't up to what they agreed to provide, it's so much easier to deal with the issue amicably when it's identified in your routine monthly meeting and immediately brought to your vendor's attention (rather than if it's allowed to go on for a lengthy period because nobody is minding your deal).

Beyond the issue of identifying minor problems while they're still minor, another issue is properly documenting the issue in the way required by your agreement. I've litigated too many cases in my time as a lawyer where I was up against a contract that says that my client should have sent a written notice of a problem within 15 days and they didn't.

They didn't because while they might have been doing a reactive so-so at best job of managing the business relationship, nobody was minding the legal side. It's asinine when you consider a company jeopardizing any legal remedies it might have in a deal because they didn't want to budget one hour per month for their tech lawyer to participate in their monthly team meeting by conference call. Crazy.

Moreover, it's not really about "legal remedies." If we're talking about legal remedies, we're talking about a seriously ill deal. Actually, what we're talking about is the concept best said by the cliché, "Good fences make for good neighbors."

As much as you want to have an informal "can't we all just be friends" relationship with your vendor, experience tells me that some level of formality is a good thing. Wait for the relationship to deteriorate before you re-involve your lawyer and an e-mail from me to your vendor is like moving your military to a higher state of alert.

The better approach is that when you notice a minor problem during your first monthly meeting, you have your lawyer send a formal notice as required by the agreement you spent days or weeks negotiating. Now, that same e-mail, and others that follow, are more like a routine diplomatic exchange.

So often, business folks are reticent to send that formal notice. Don't be. It's the procedure everybody agreed to in the agreement, so use it. If you don't, you may unintentionally waive rights you had under the agreement and send the message to the vendor that you'll let things slide.

The right message is we're watching closely, we expect you to do what you said you would do exactly as you said you would—and in return, you'll just love how our progress payments arrive like magic—right on time.

DOCUMENT RETENTION POLICIES

Seemingly innocuous documents can haunt your company in a courtroom. The best defense is destroying documents. If you do it right, you're legal and safe. If you get it wrong, you may find a judge accusing you of destroying relevant evidence. The answer is a well-formulated document retention policy (DRP).

While I admit that nobody will ever win a business leadership and vision award from the Chamber of Commerce for giving time and attention to the development of a DRP, you need to do it. It's like sleep. You may not feel like it's productive time, but you shouldn't try to live without it.

Especially with information going digital and the price of digital storage on its way down, it's too easy to keep everything. The problem with that approach is that when you're involved in litigation, you're almost inviting the other side to go fishing through your ancient records. Who knows what evil lurks there?

It only gets worse when you're faced with a subpoena for a document and you have so much data that you can't even find what you need to find. Now, you look recalcitrant. (Throughout this chapter, I'm going to use the word document broadly to mean any type of record, whether written, digital, audio, visual or whatever).

Let's start with what you wish your DRP could say, but can't. "When litigation is threatened or filed, immediately review all relevant documents. Upon completion of the review, destroy all documents that are detrimental to our position."

Somehow, this policy conjures up something having to do with 18 minutes of tape. Let's just say that it didn't work for Nixon and it won't work for you.

No matter what your policy is, it must call for a complete halt to document destruction once litigation is threatened or filed.

If you ignore this rule, you may find yourself accused of spoliation. "Spoliation" can be loosely defined as the intentional and wrongful destruction of evidence that is material to an ongoing or imminent litigation matter. If a court feels that you're guilty of spoliation, it has many weapons at its disposal if it wants to sanction you. You don't want to go there.

It's an ugly place to be. In creating your DRP, you're going to have to assemble a team which should consist of a high level executive responsible for the project, your chief information officer (CIO), department heads, tax counsel, regulatory counsel, and legal counsel. Ultimately, the CEO should be the one to sign off on the DRP. You need the CIO because one of the considerations is the technological feasibility of what it is you want to do.

An important issue is to what extent can you safely and effectively automate the process. You need department heads so that they have an opportunity to comment on the unique document retention needs of their department.

Your tax and regulatory counsel are there because of tax laws, and if you're in a regulated industry, then those regulations may also impose some very specific requirements. The first principle is that you should be sure to keep everything needed to successfully run your business. This is a pure business issue. What do you need and how long do you need it?

The second principle is that you should never destroy anything that the law requires you to keep. This principle requires you to stop all document destruction once somebody threatens or commences litigation or other legal proceedings against you. You can start again only with the approval of your lawyer.

Subject to the second principle, tax law and regulatory requirements, the general rule is that you can destroy your documents anytime you want. Having said that, if a court ever puts your destruction of documents under scrutiny, it looks much better if you did the destruction in a systematic way based on a schedule and a documented DRP.

It's common sense. If you destroy all e-mail when it's six months old, it's hard to accuse you of spoliation because a year-old e-mail is long gone. If you suddenly have a DRP in place the day before a lawsuit is filed—well, you get the picture.

One pitfall to avoid in creating your DRP is not taking into account the fact that most documents have multiple copies. You have to consider your employees' personal files, local hard drives, and backups. It doesn't help to destroy working data if you keep your backups forever.

Dealing with backups will probably require your CIO to create backups with the DRP in mind. Depending upon the media that you use for the backup, it may not be possible to selectively destroy parts of the backup. This creates a problem for you if your DRP requires you to destroy e-mail after six months but tax records after seven years, yet they both reside on the same tape.

If you think that the prospect of creating a DRP sounds like a boring and thankless task, you're probably right. It is boring and thankless. Still, the penalty for not dealing with the issue could be a long-forgotten memo rising up from the depths to hurt you in a courtroom.

Chapter Ten

History, Background,
Thoughts, and Legal Considerations

THE FILM INDUSTRY, NAPSTER, AND
FILE SHARING ONLINE

It cries of First Amendment freedom from all parties concerned.

With all of the attention that was focused on the controversy between the music industry and Napster, it was easy to overlook the fact that the film industry was also immersed in a legal battle that could have ultimately decided how and if we use the Internet to distribute file-sharing software.

Ironically, the film industry's litigation had the makings of a great film. It involved two states (California and New York), both businesses and individuals alike, and cries of First Amendment freedom from all parties concerned. The case became one of the hottest cases in the film industry since it tried to block the sale of VCRs in the mid-1980s.

The controversy began when Jon Johansen, a 16-year-old Norwegian, created the Decode Copy Scrambling System (DeCSS), which is software that breaks through the copy protection code used to prevent you from copying movies on DVD. When you use it "properly," DeCSS creates an unprotected version of a DVD movie, which you can then easily transmit over the Internet, à la Napster.

After Johansen created DeCSS, he posted the code on his father's website. (Ah, those crazy kids.) Other websites began to link to the code, and soon DeCSS started to appear on hard drives across the world.

Of course, this didn't sit well with the film industry, which had seen how ugly the Napster situation became. One trade group, the DVD Copy Control Association, promptly filed suit in California to stop numerous websites from linking to or posting the DeCSS code. The brunt of the Association's claim was that the defendants were violating the Digital Millennium Copyright Act (DMCA), a 1998 law that prohibits the distribution of products that can circumvent copy protection schemes. In an initial blow to the film industry, however, the California court declined to rule against the websites.

Then, just like a Clint Eastwood western, after the court rejected the association's attempt to "restore order," in walked the big gun, the Motion Picture Association of America.

The MPAA sauntered into a federal courthouse in New York and filed a similar lawsuit against the websites, but this time included Johansen as a defendant. Perhaps not coincidentally, 10 days after the MPAA filed its lawsuit, the police raided Johansen's home and seized his computer equipment.

The MPAA's argument was simple, but effective: Since the sole purpose of DeCSS was to break through copy protection of DVD movies, the defendants were clearly violating the provisions of the DMCA.

At first blush, the MPAA's argument is strong. The DMCA is clearly meant to ban the distribution of code that encourages online theft of intellectual property, and DeCSS fits neatly into that outlawed category. Since, traditionally, the government has been allowed to ban certain products that are used primarily for illegal purposes, DeCSS might be properly banned as well.

On the other hand, Johansen and his posse also presented a compelling argument. In sum, they claimed that DeCSS is nothing more than Johansen's speech, albeit expressed in a digitized form, comprised of ones and zeros.

While the court agreed that DeCSS was a form of expression, it nevertheless ruled in favor of the MPAA, and held that the expressive aspect of the DeCSS code "no more immunizes its functional aspects from regulation than the expressive motives of an assassin immunizes the assassin's action." Accordingly, the court ordered the immediate halt to any further distribution of DeCSS.

But our story doesn't end there. Johansen and his crew have appealed, and a federal appellate court has now requested that each party answer a series of written questions related to the impact that the lower court's ruling had on the First Amendment.

Although a decision from the appellate court will likely come later this year, no matter how the court rules, the U.S. Supreme Court will likely get involved.

Pass the popcorn, please.

VOTING OVER THE INTERNET

We've all heard the jokes about how Florida handled the presidential election. You know the ones like, "How come them old folks can do eight bingo cards at one time, but can't handle one ballot?"

One solution suggested to the problems created by our antiquated voting system is voting over the Internet. The problem is that it's just not ready for prime time. (If you keep reading, I promise that you won't see anything about hanging or pregnant you know whats.)

Clearly, Internet voting could be an improvement over lots of methods now used throughout the country and light years ahead of the punch cards that we use in South Florida. Just as clear is that Internet voting is rife with its own legal and practical problems.

Political science types (yes, I was a political science not computer science major before law school) list at least five key attributes to ensure a free and fair election. Take a deep breath and here's the list: transparency, security, secrecy, timeliness, and equity.

Any reasonable method used at a public polling place wins on transparency when compared to Net voting. Voting is "transparent" when partisans can watch ballots from the moment that they're issued to the moment they're counted. While computerized audit trails may some day serve this purpose, the issue of "security" causes people not to trust computerized audit trails.

Today, we live in a world where we regularly read stories about major companies and government agencies being victimized by hacking and other types of computer crime. This doesn't exactly engender trust in the idea of using the Internet to choose a president.

Another big security issue is ensuring that the Internet voter is who he or she purports to be. In Chicago, they used to say, "Vote early and often." Unless we solve the security issues with Net voting, we might have to change that to "Vote early and remember that your computer doesn't need to stop for bathroom breaks."

Secrecy is a tough one. Computers are all about retaining information. If you vote online, the simple fact is that it may be possible for somebody to trace your vote back to you. Still, if you take "secrecy" to its logical extreme, you could point out that your ballot card has your fingerprints on it.

The Net is a winner when it comes to timeliness. It was a bad joke to think that in 2000 we had to wait 10 days after Election Day to total the foreign absentee ballots. With Net voting, votes will be instantly cast and counted.

For many people, "equity" is a big hurdle with Internet voting. I think it's a red herring. Here, we get into digital divide issues about how less advantaged people have less access to computers. While that's true, they also have less access to cars to drive to voting places. Life is never perfectly fair.

No matter what system we use for voting, it will always be better for one group than another.

Net voting may help the homebound and disabled while not helping the poor or those who choose not to own computers. No matter what system we use, we'll need to have more than one way to vote because no system is perfect for everybody.

Nationally, we rely today on some odd mix of punch cards, voting machines, hand written ballots, computers, mail-in ballots, and other methods. Maybe part of the answer is to make Net voting an option, but not a requirement. If we did that, we could certainly reduce the number of physical polling places while making use of the latest technology.

Now that I've discussed some of the many flaws with an Internet-based voting system, the obvious question becomes, what do we do to improve voting methods. Of course, the answer is—use the Internet.

I'm convinced that we can solve all the problems with online voting to our reasonable satisfaction. I emphasize the word "reasonable" because no system is perfect and all too often, we refuse to adopt a computerized system to replace a traditional system because the hi-tech solution isn't perfect. Well, the traditional system isn't perfect either.

While new systems often create new problems, we should adopt new systems whenever they provide a cost-effective net improvement over the old way.

Do you think that most people will be voting from home in 2050? I suspect that most people believe that they will. If that's the case, I'd like to suggest that we invest the money to develop those improved systems sooner and not later.

NANOTECHNOLOGY

"Nanotechnology" is the science of very small things and I mean very small. Like every new technology that preceded it, the development of the law surrounding nanotechnology is well behind the advances in the technology. The law in this area is where Internet Law was in 1995. It fills only a pamphlet.

According to the Nanobusiness Alliance, a more precise definition of nanotechnology is "the ability to do things—measure, see, predict and make—on the scale of atoms and molecules. Traditionally, the nanotechnology realm is defined as being between 0.1 and 100 nanometers, a nanometer being one thousandth of a micron (micrometer), which is, in turn, one thousandth of a millimeter." Some speculate that nanotechnology, or simply nanotech, may be the next big thing in the world of technology, following a list that includes the industrial revolution, atomic energy, computers, space, the Internet and now, nanotech.

To help you understand just how small is small, consider this: A nanometer is one-billionth of a meter, which is approximately 1/80,000 the width of a human hair and 10 times the diameter of a hydrogen atom. The size of a nanometer relative to the width of the human hair is comparable to relating 6.5 feet to 100 miles. A nanometer is roughly the width of four atoms.

With nanotech, we're talking about working on the atomic and molecular level to create things that have unique chemical, physical, and biological properties because of their nano size. In a sense, nanotechnology mirrors the workings of living cells, which manufacture with atomic precision.

Nanotech cuts across many disciplines, including chemistry, physics, biology, computer science, and engineering. It's gone from Star Trek to an industry that receives more than half a billion dollars a year from the U.S. government.

If you think that nanotech is just hype, consider that companies like IBM, HP, TI, GM, GE, Siemens, Intel, Hitachi, and Dow are involved in nanotechnology R&D. Furthermore, the U.S. is getting stiff foreign competition from the usual suspects including Japan, the EU, Russia, Korea, and China. Unfortunately, some believe that they are ahead of the U.S. is some ways.

Also, President Bush's proposed 2004 budget provides $847 million for the multi-agency National Nanotechnology Initiative (NNI). This is a 9.5% increase over 2003.

According to the President's Office of Science and Technology Policy (OSTP), this money "will advance fundamental understanding of the nanoscale phenomena—unique properties of matter that occur at the level of clusters of atoms and molecules. This increased understanding promises to underlie revolutionary advances that will contribute to improvements in medicine, manufacturing, high-performance materials, information technology, and environmental technologies."

Interestingly, the most significant increases are for the Department of Energy (DOE) and the National Science Foundation (NSF). According to the OSTP, "NSF continues to have the largest share of federal nanotechnology funding, reflecting the broad mission of NSF in supporting fundamental research across all disciplines of science and engineering. The request for DOE's nanotechnology program reflects, in part, the development of five geographically distributed user centers."

The OSTP goes on to say that examples of notable achievement over the past year include "the development of single molecule electron devices, molecular motors, nanoscale fabrication using atomic force microprobes, micro-cantilevers to detect proteins, and enhanced medical imaging using nanoparticle-based probes." It's not just Star Trek and science fiction anymore.

On the legislative front, Representative Mike Honda (D-San Jose) introduced the Nanoscience and Nanotechnology Advisory Board Act of 2003. The legislation would establish an independent advisory board, comprised of leaders from industry and academia, advising the President and Congress on research investment strategy, policy, and objectives.

Further, the legislation would create an advisory board who would determine short-term, medium-range, and longer-range goals and objectives, and performance metrics. The bill calls for the board to submit an annual report to the President and Congress describing the progress made with nanotechnology.

The bill is probably a step in the right direction in that its underlying purpose would seem to be to begin to focus policy-making attention in the area of nanotech. That has to be a good idea when there has really been so little focus on the many issues raised by nanotech.

The issues raised start at the ethical and moral, and work their way right into legal issues. For example, if nanotech could allow us to go into genes and fix them to prevent disease, is it okay to go into genes to "improve" genes that have no obvious problems?

You then go from the high-level ethical, moral, and legal issues right into practical business issues. As lawyers inevitably get involved in what will undoubtedly be a high-stakes business, all sorts of patent, copyright, health, safety, environmental, and other legal issues arise. Then once you create the nanotech devices, you have business issues involving turning the devices into profitable inventions and businesses.

As this all goes from science fiction to reality, I look forward to negotiating more and more of the licensing and technology transfer deals that will certainly arise.

CLIENTS BEWARE: LAWYERS TELL JOKES TOO

We've all heard our share of lawyer jokes over the years. I'll tell you a secret. Lawyers tell client jokes.

Here's one of my favorites:

A man in a hot air balloon is lost. He reduces the balloon's height and spots a man below. He shouts, "Excuse me, can you tell me where I am?"

The man below says: "Yes, you're in a hot air balloon hovering at 30 feet."

"You must be a lawyer," says the balloonist.

"I am," replies the man. "How did you know?"

"Well," says the balloonist, "everything you have told me is technically correct, but useless."

The man below says, "You must work in business."

"I do," replies the balloonist, "but how did you know?"

"Well," says the lawyer, "you don't know where you are, or where you're going, but you expect me to be able to help. You're in the same position you were before we met, but now it's my fault."

Both client and lawyer jokes are funny, but what's not amusing or useful are the culture and communications gaps brought to the fore by the humor.

The two sides don't understand each other. Business folks don't care about terms and conditions of website use. They're not interested in the niceties of an arbitration clause or warranty provision. What they want to know about is how do these things protect their business interests.

It's like fuel injection in a car. Most of us don't ever think about fuel injection, don't want to think about fuel injection, and don't care to change our blissful state of ignorance about fuel injection. The experts decided that it's an improvement over carburetors and will make our cars run better. The "run better" part is all that matters to us.

For some reason, this is lost on many lawyers. Lawyers seem to think that most of the world cares about the technical side of what they do. The fact is that they don't. Most people want to know the bottom line and hate the way lawyers can talk in circles.

Business folks don't care about the law of domain-name disputes. They want to know if they can register the dotcom version of a name and not be sued. They want to know what steps they need to take to protect themselves. They want answers.

The point is that from the client's perspective it's not about the law, it's about business.

If you use your lawyers properly and they do their job, it's about mitigating risk, solving business problems, and making money.

Call for a Truce

I'm not going to try to take on the entire battlefield of the lawyer-client culture gap. It's too big. Instead, I'm going to address this culture gap in my niche area of technology law.

I'm going to point out that tech lawyers tend to be more entrepreneurial and younger—not too many 50 and 60-something-year-old tech lawyers around, for obvious reasons.

Entrepreneurial is the nature of the beast because of the personality type this niche attracts. Our culture gap is naturally narrower. Let's recognize that and use it to our mutual benefit.

When I tell you that your million-dollar tech deal will take more than a week to negotiate and document, and that your fee will be measured in the many thousands not the many hundreds, I'd like to suggest that you be open-minded to the fact that the deal may be more complex than you realize.

You're like the lost balloonist and it's not my "fault" that your deal will take 30 pages to explain. If that's a problem for you, then scratch it out yourself and good luck.

I've seen clients come and go with the economic winds of the tech bubble and bust cycle. We're on the same side. I'm always telling my clients that I need and want them to succeed. Their success is my success. We should be enjoying the benefits of a symbiotic relationship.

One of the worst effects of the culture gap is that business folks wait until the last second before they involve their lawyer. The fact is that tech deals take time. They're as inherently complex as the technology that underlies them.

Let's make a new deal. Let some entrepreneurial tech lawyer somewhere show you his stuff early in a deal when he can make a real difference. Give him the time he needs to do his job properly. Let's have no more lawyers talking in circles. Last, but not least, no more lawyer or client jokes—just a profitable deal for everyone.

Index

About the Author

Mark Grossman is a shareholder and chairs Technology Law Group of the law firm Becker & Poliakoff. A 1982 cum laude graduate of the Georgetown University Law Center in Washington, D.C., the focus of his practice since about 1990 has been Technology Law.

Mark is a much sought-after speaker, having spoken at hundreds of conferences over the years. He is also among the most prolific writers in his field.

He has written the Miami Herald's "TechLaw" column since 2000 and prior to that wrote for publications like *PC World* and Washington's *Legal Times*.

Mark was appointed a subject matter expert to the State of Florida's Internet Task Force, has served on the Advisory Board of BNA's *Electronic Commerce & Law Newsletter* and the Board of Editors of *The Internet Newsletter*, a publication of Law Journal Newsletters.

In 2002, Mark was chosen to appear in the 2003–2004 edition of *The Best Lawyers in America* (www.bestlawyers.com). Inclusion in this work is determined by an election in which only lawyers participate.